# ORIGA… S



# & WREATHS

## A Kaleidoscope of 28 Decorative Origami Creations

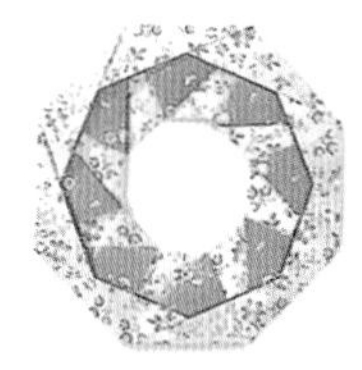
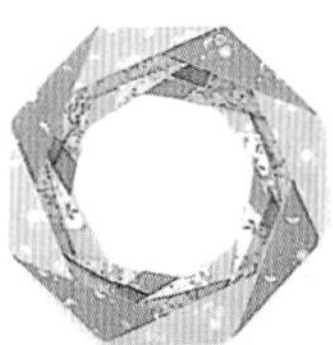
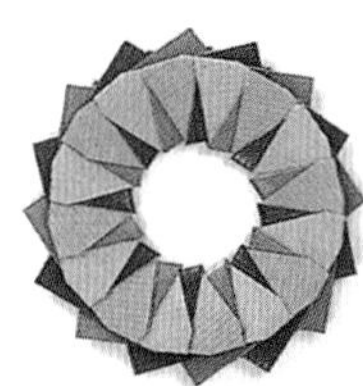

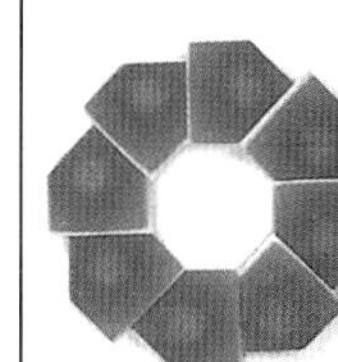

Introduced in this book is a collection of rings and wreaths that are made of unit origami. Please make use of them for Christmas decorations, brooches, earrings and other ornaments. But these are not the goals of this unit origami. The very essence is the pleasure of folding, joining and completing the rings. It is also interesting to enjoy the dramatic changes of impressions which brought about by different color arrangements.
The simple and clear instructions are so easy to follow that even absolute beginners can make them in a few steps without confusion. There are not many units to make, so you can readily get to work. They will reveal a kaleidoscopic world of rings.

Tomoko Fuse

50 RING 1

51 RING 2

53 RING 3

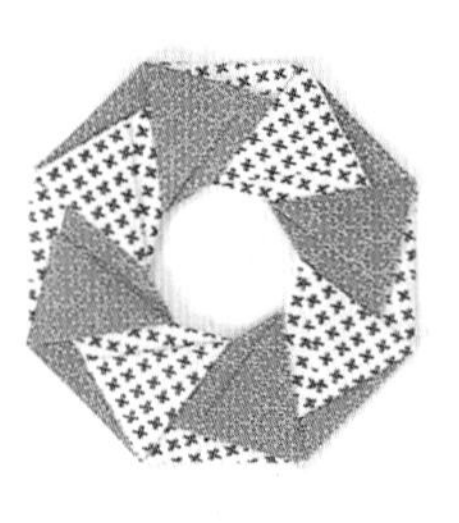

54 RING 4

55 RING 5

56 RING 6

58 RING 7

60 RING 8

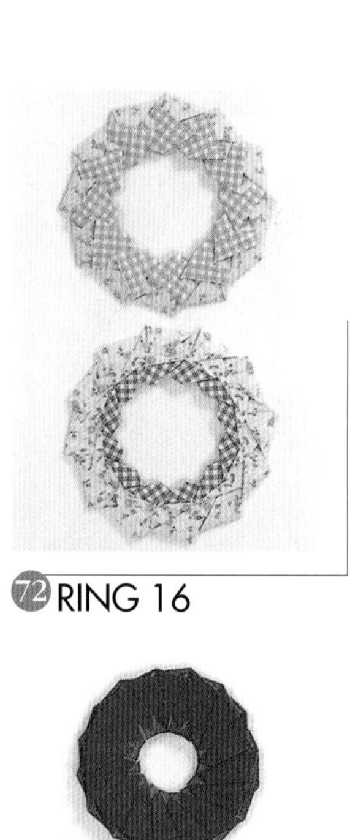
72 RING 16

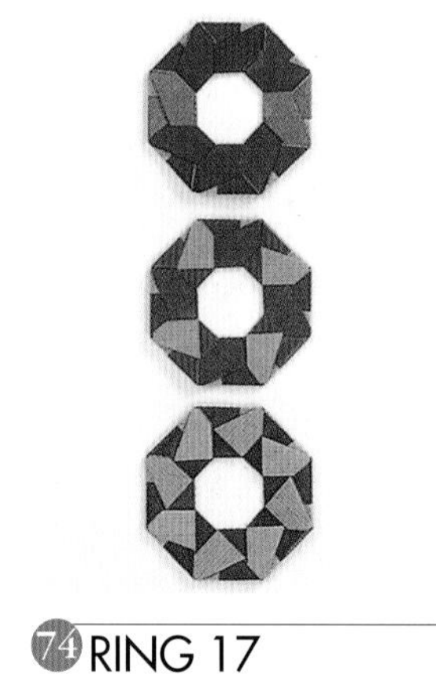
74 RING 17

75 RING 18

77 RING 19

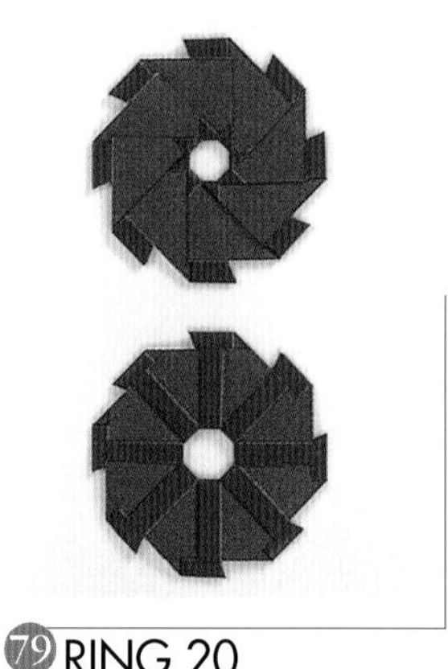
79 RING 20

80 RING 21

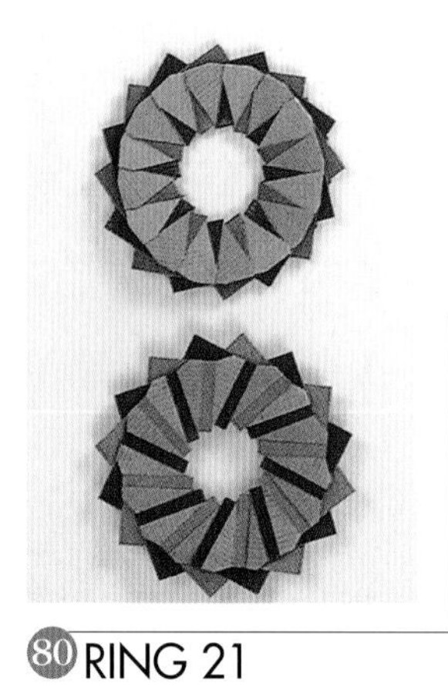
80 RING 21

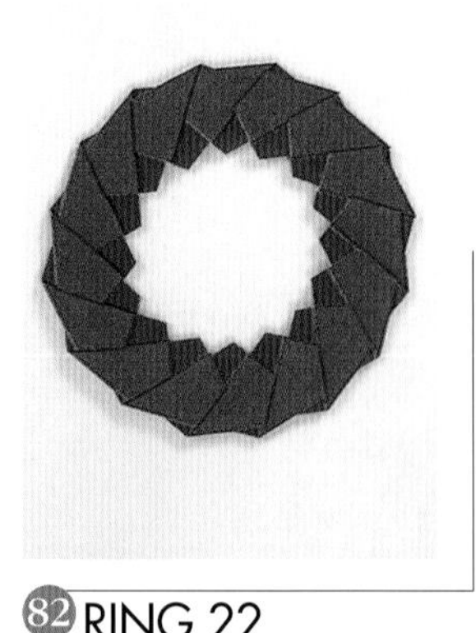
82 RING 22

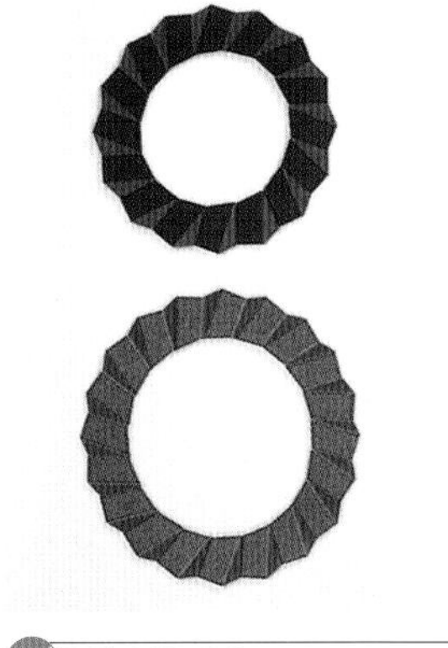

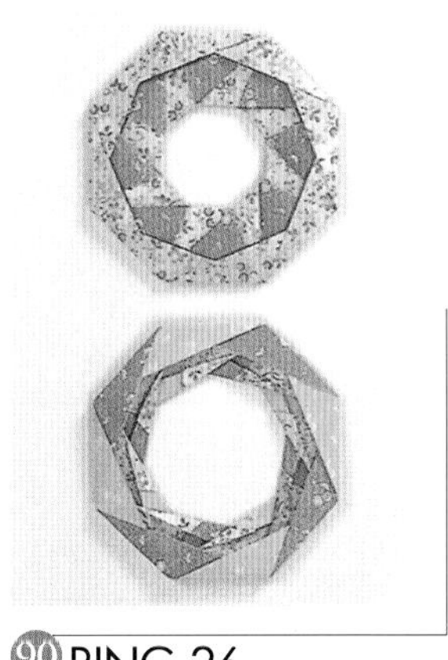

# Ring 1 p50
# 28 p92

Ring 1 p50

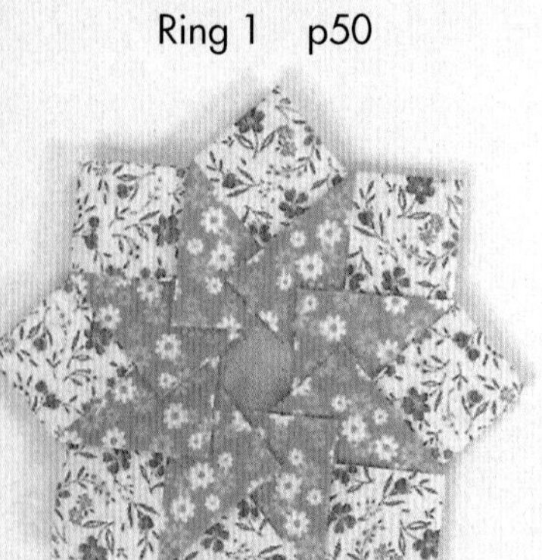
Ring 1 p50

Ring 28-B p92

Graceful rings made of paper which has floral patterns on both sides.

Ring 28-A p92

Ring 28-C p92

Ring 1 p50

Ring 2 p51
7 p58
12 p66

Ring 2 p51

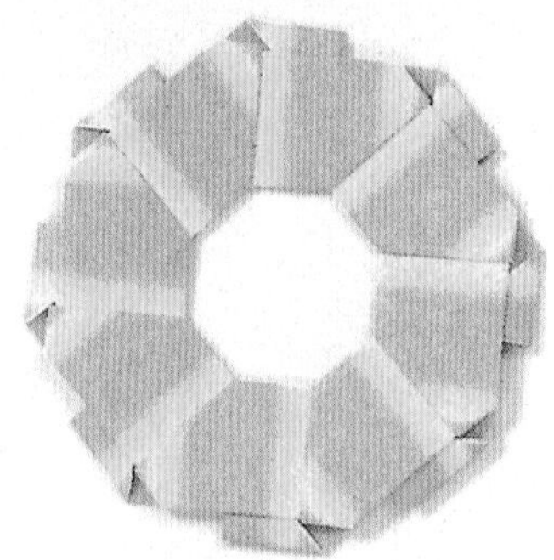

Ring 2 p51

Ring 12 p66

Ring 7 p58

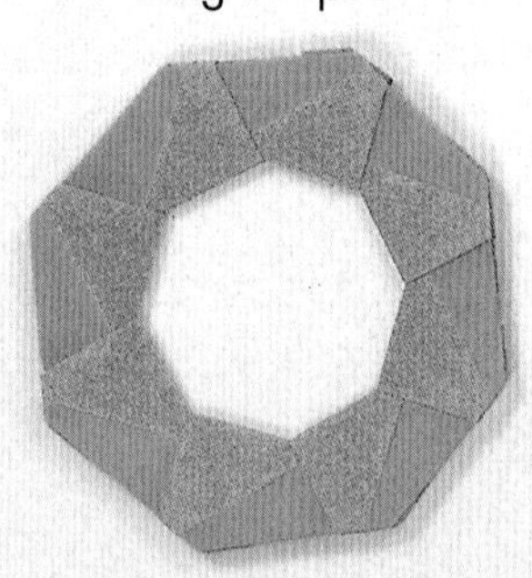

An American friend gave me a lot of paper of blurred patterns made in Korea, and I made use of them. These rings might be good for coasters.

Ring 2　p51

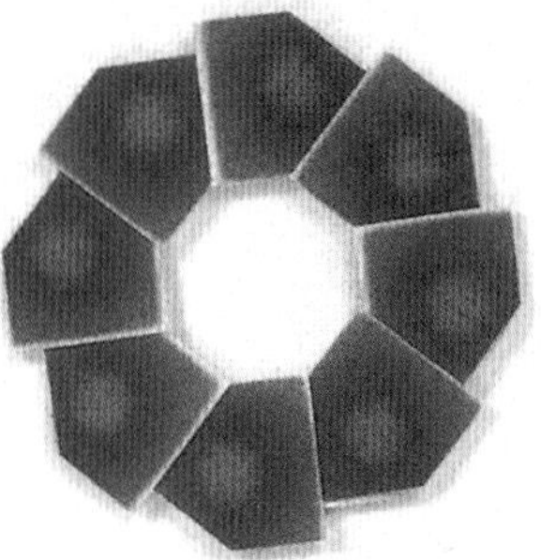

Ring 12　p66

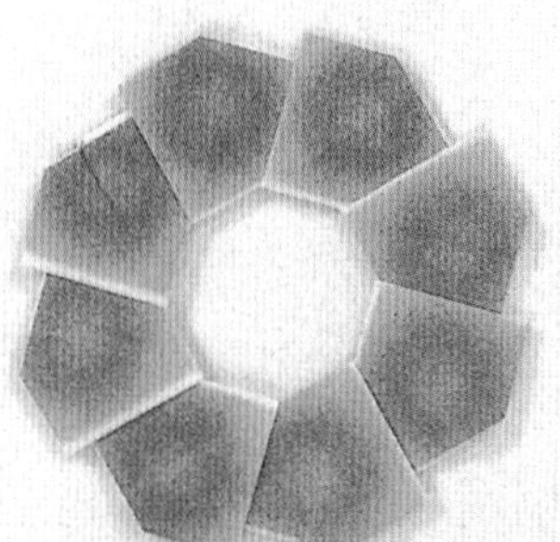

Ring 2　p51

## Ring 4 p54
## 11 p65

Ring 4 p54

Ring 4 p54

Ring 11 p65

Rings made of glittering paper. Although the folding methods are the same, the impression becomes different, depending on the paper.

# Ring 2 p51

Paper of fine patterns is refined and elegant.
Characteristically, it is also pleasant to the touch.

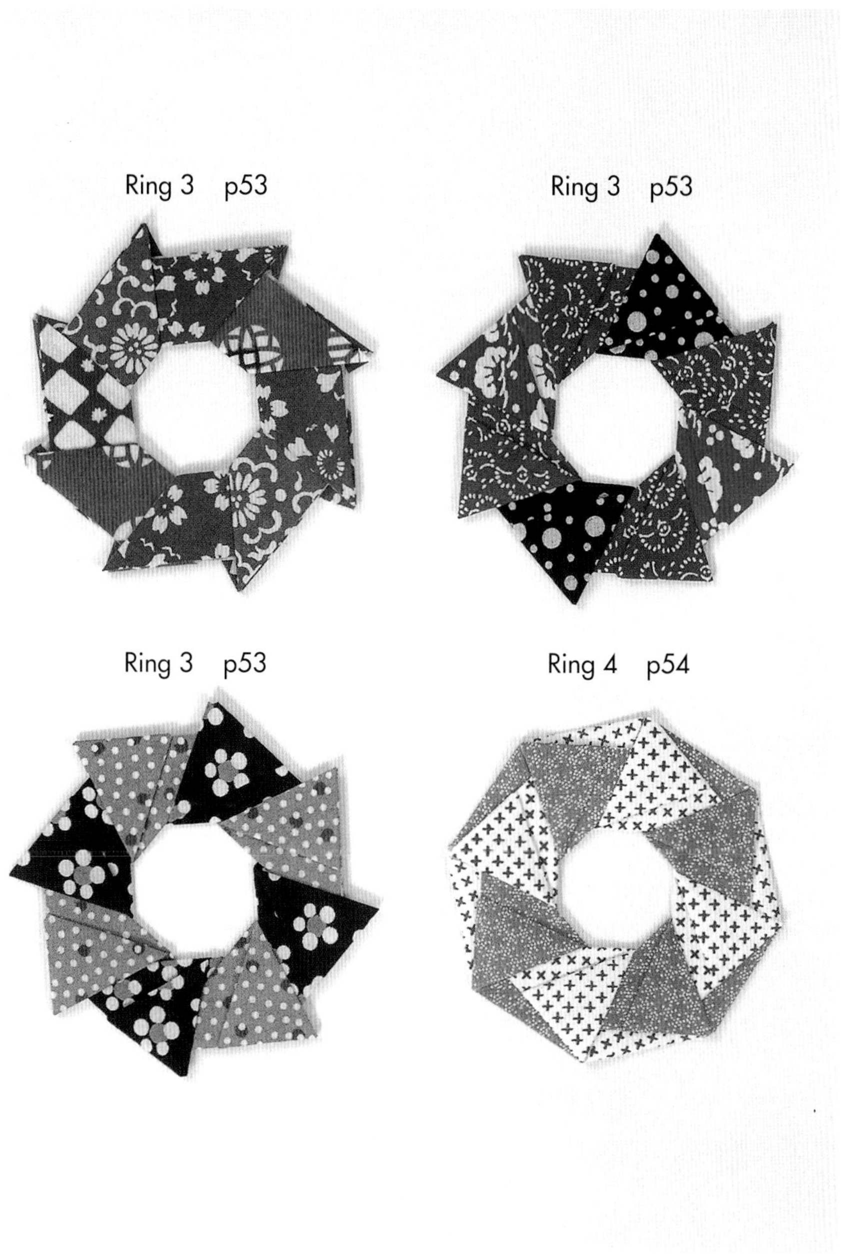


It is hard to dispose of scraps of Japanese paper.
They are right materials for making rings.

Ring 6 p56

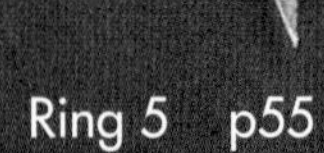
Ring 5 p55

Ring 5 p55

How do you use these glittering rings?

# Ring 26-A, B p90

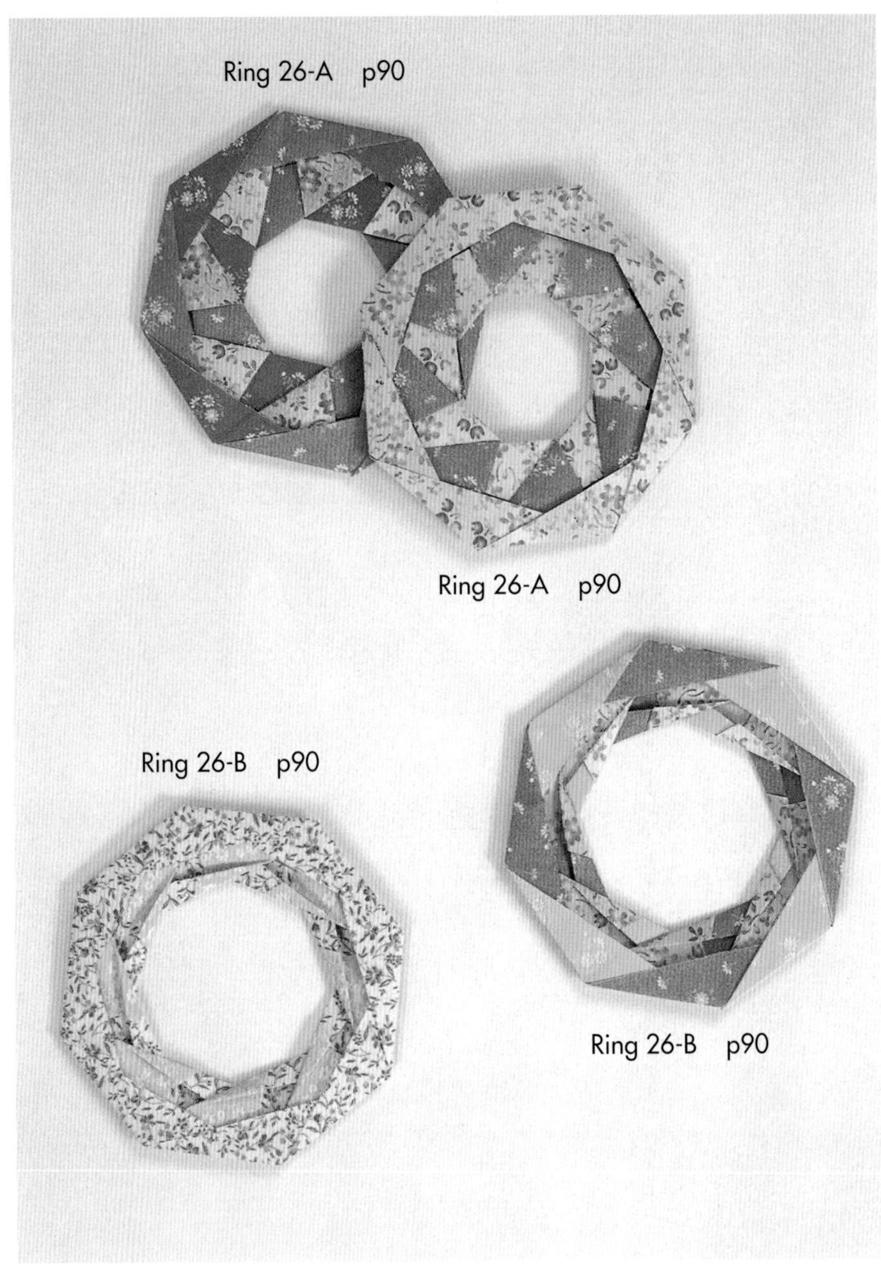


Color combinations are always difficult problems.
Anyway try to make as many rings as possible.

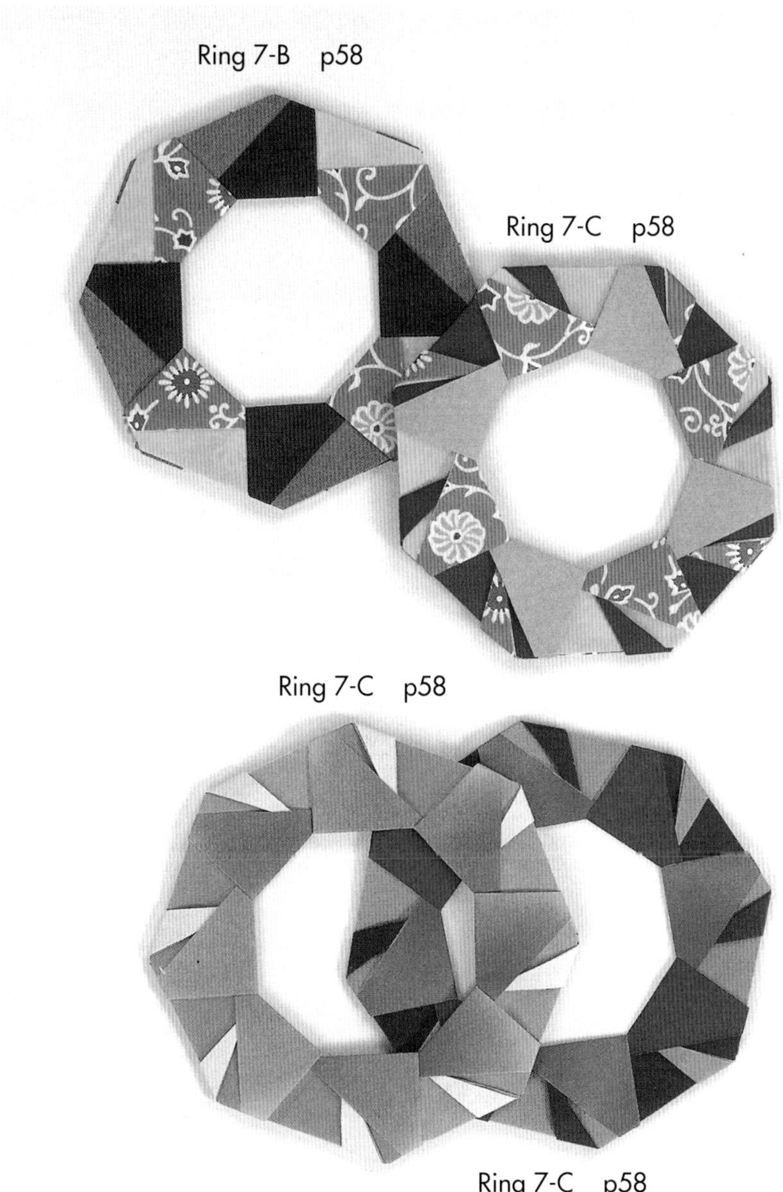


When folded and joined, the impression of paper becomes different from that of the original. Sometimes I feel happy and sometimes I am disappointed.

# Ring 13 p68

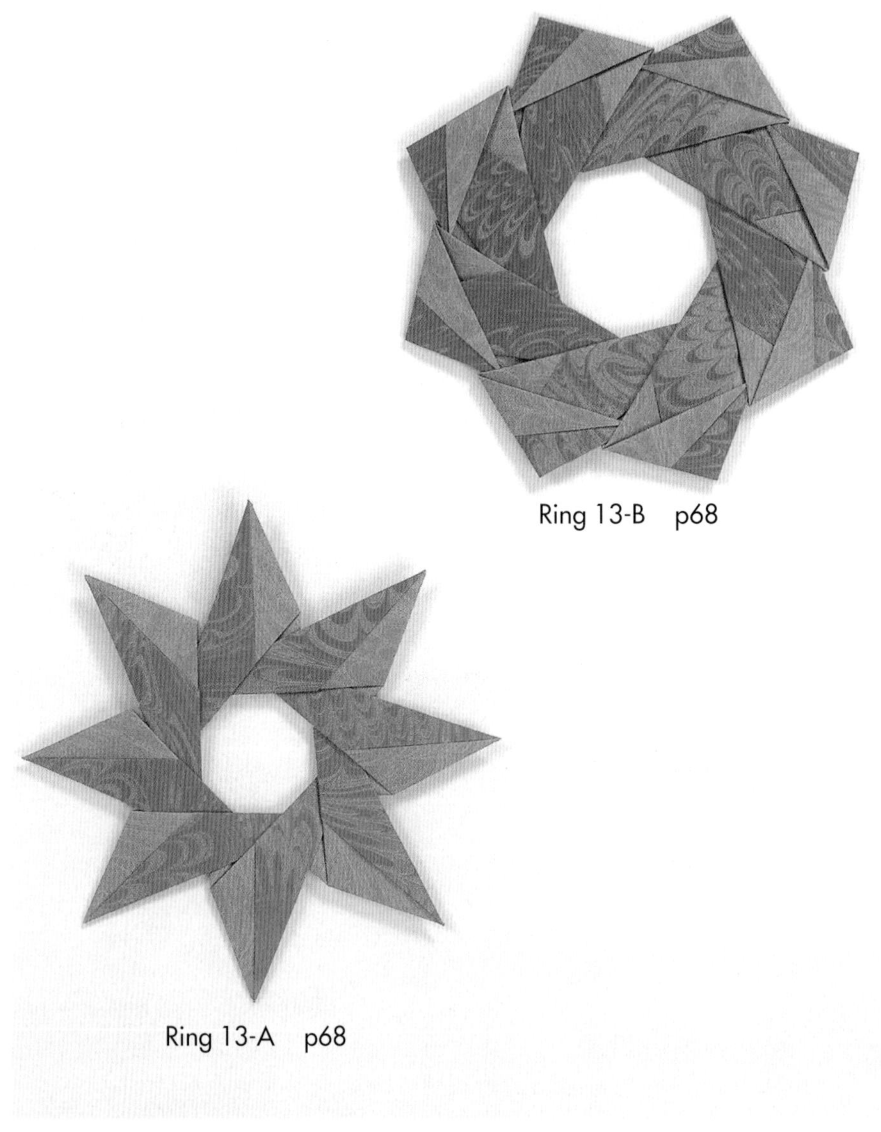

Ring 13-B p68

Ring 13-A p68

These chic rings are made of paper with marbling patterns on both sides.

It is interesting to see a thick ring from the side.
This might be used for a pot stand.

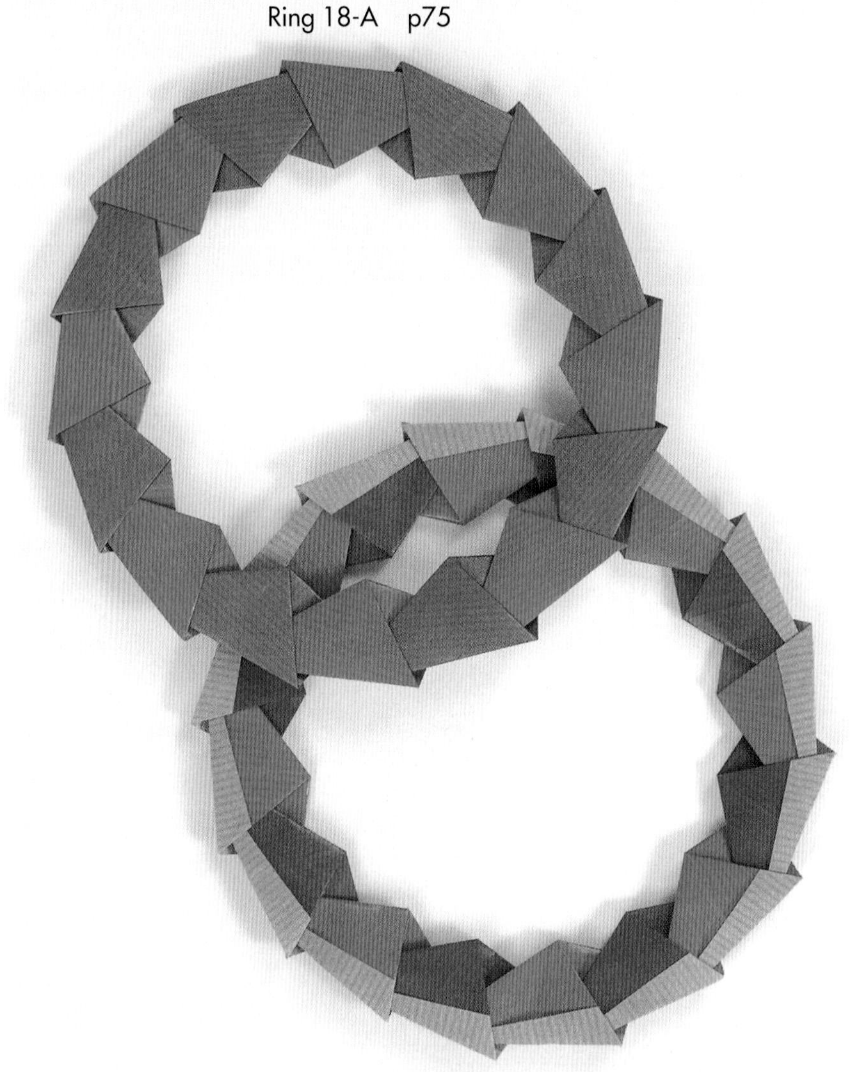

Ring 18-A p75

Ring 18-B p75

You can make a clear folding line on kraft paper, so it is always pleasant to fold the paper.

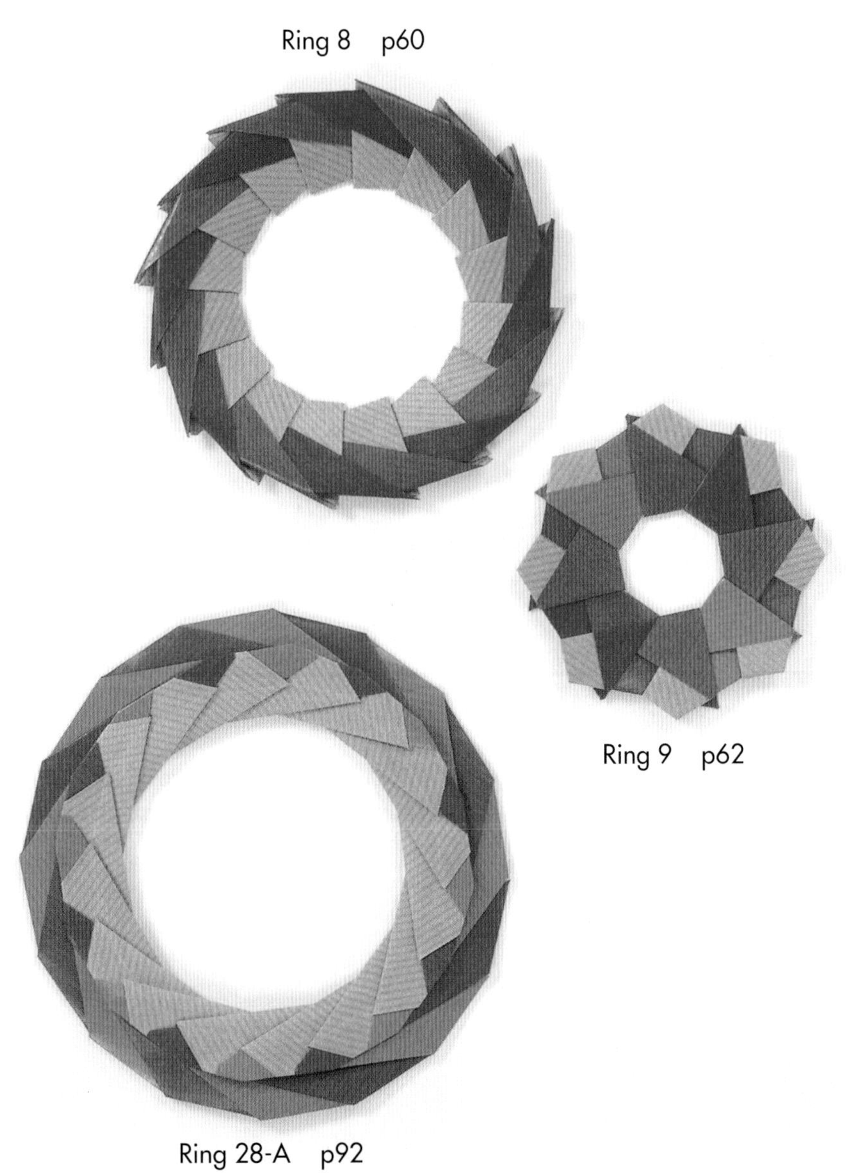

Ring 8 p60

Ring 9 p62

Ring 28-A p92

# Ring 17 p74

Ring 17-B p74

Ring 17-mixed p74

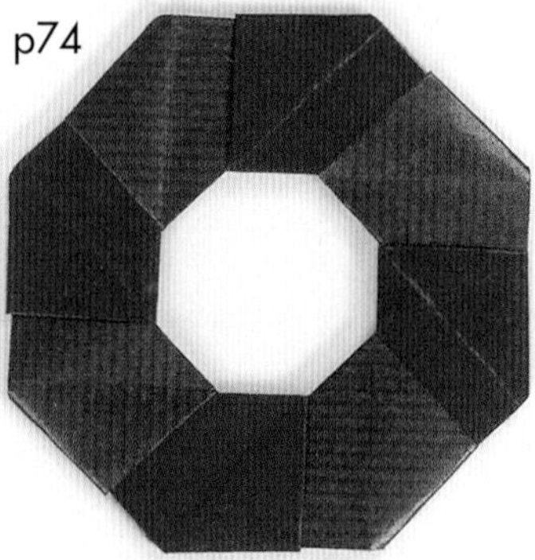

Ring 17-A p74

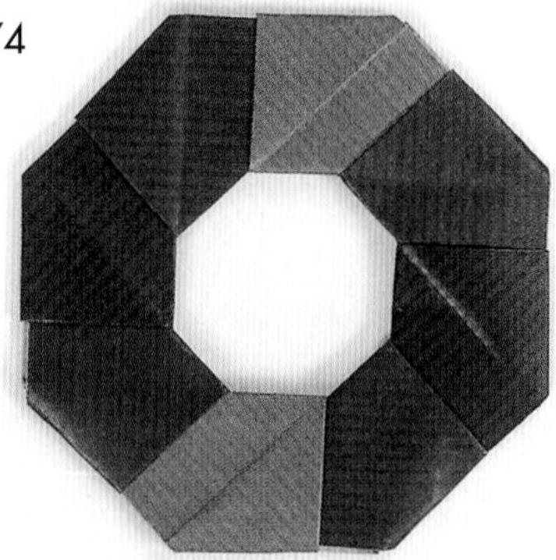

Simple rings made of craft paper.

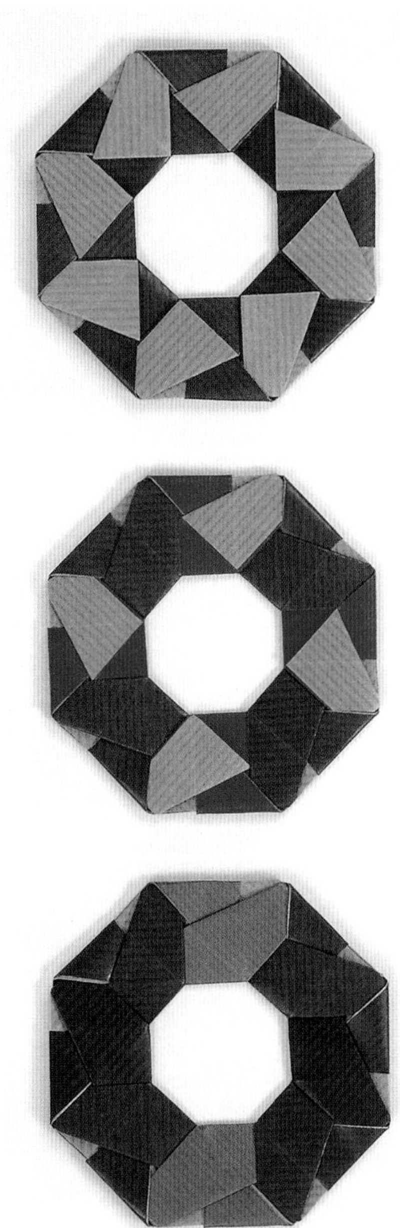

The back of the left rings has a variety of patterns like these.

# Ring 16 p72

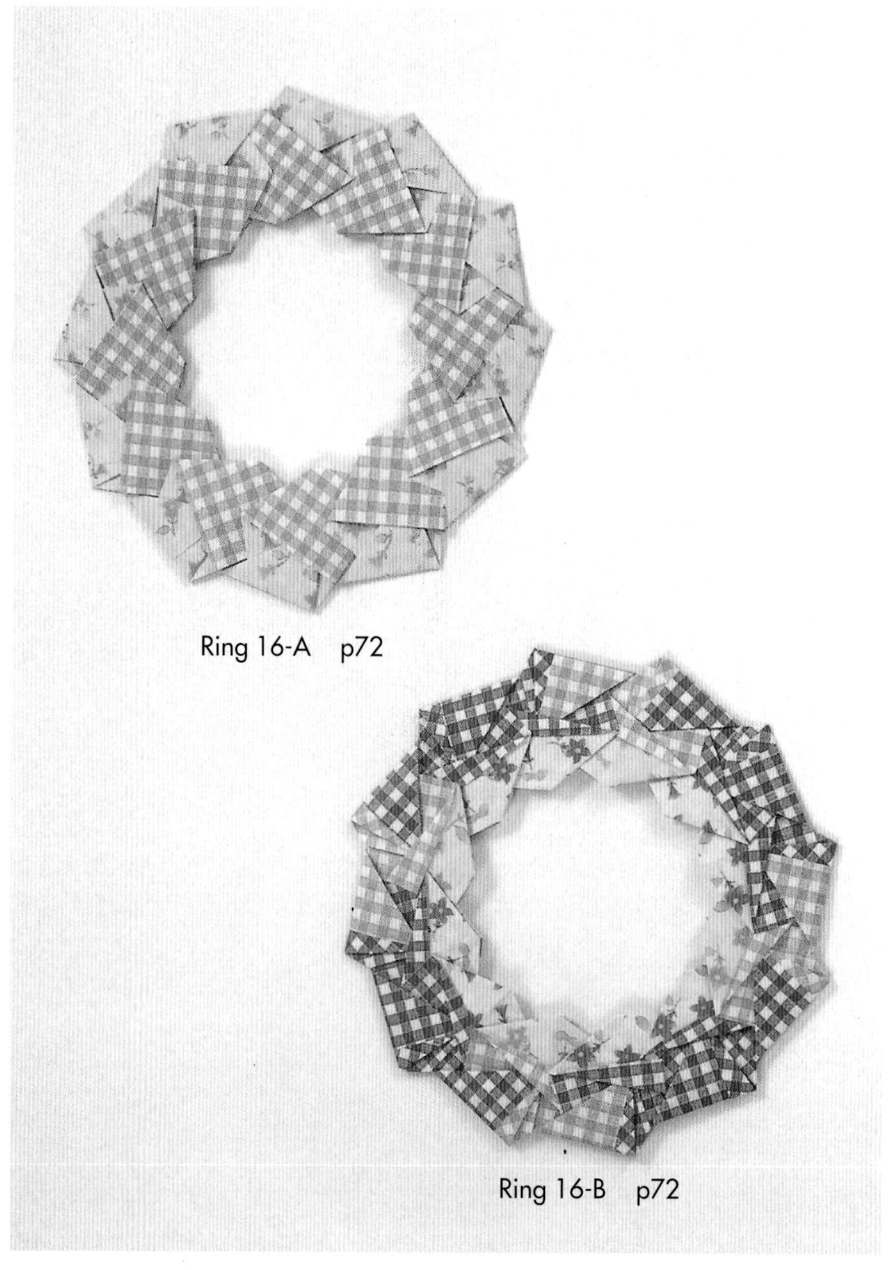

Ring 16-A p72

Ring 16-B p72

The rings made of patterned paper have inconspicuous looks, but they are bright and cheerful.

The patterns of the front and back are different.
The impression changes, depending on paper used.

# Ring 25-A (The back side is shown in the circle.) p88

This ring is made of tracing paper with fine uneven wave patterns. It is exciting to fold, imaging how the completed work would come out.

Ring 24-B p86

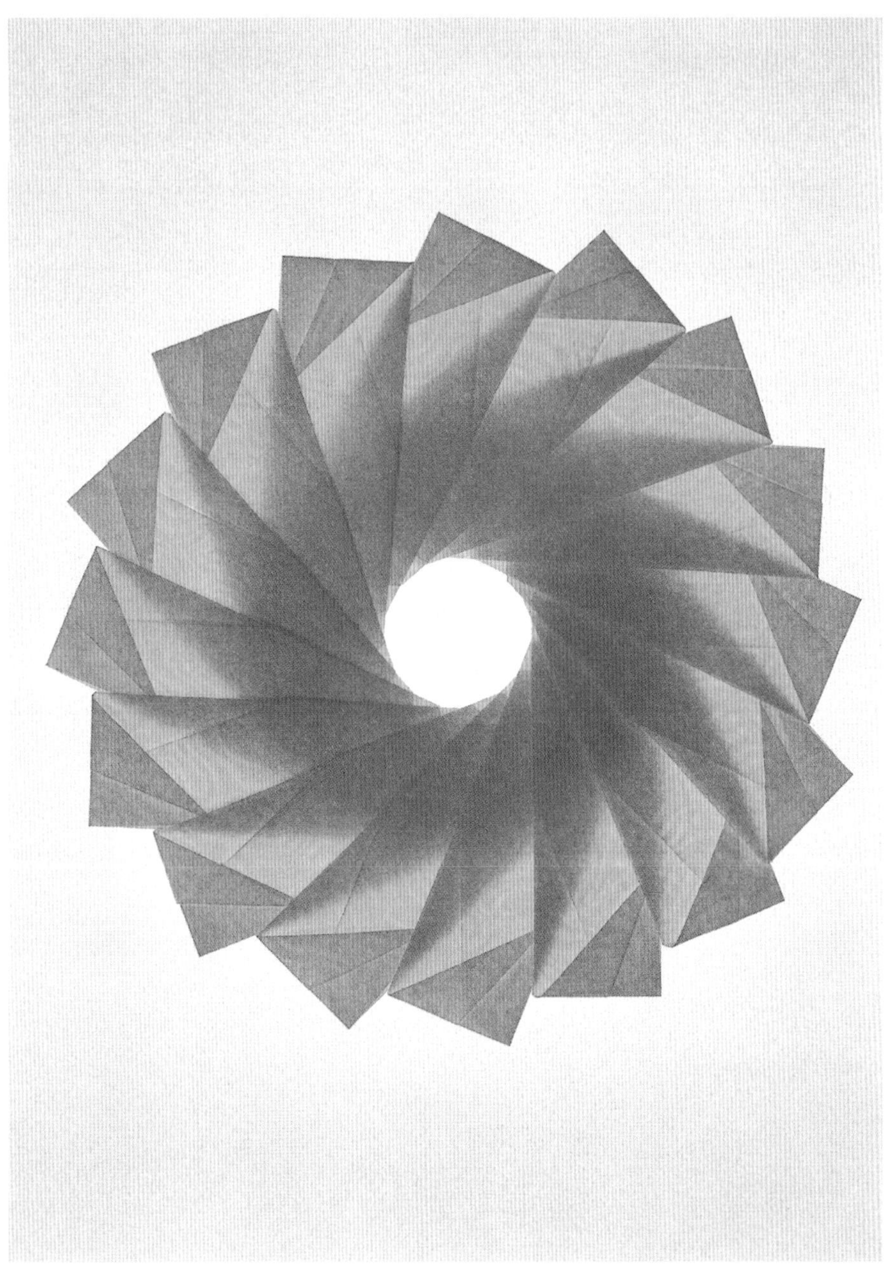

# Ring 16-A p72
# 25-A p88

Ring 16-A p72

Ring 25-A p88

This is a beautiful harmony of light and paper.
Another face of the ring.

Ring 6　p56

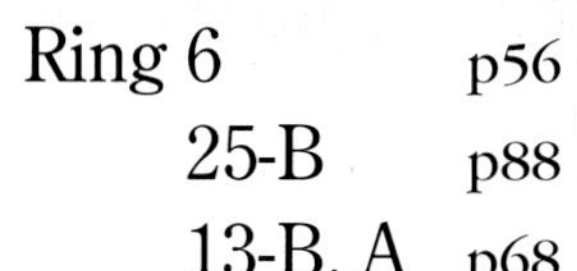

Ring 6　p56
25-B　p88
13-B, A　p68

Ring 13-B　p68

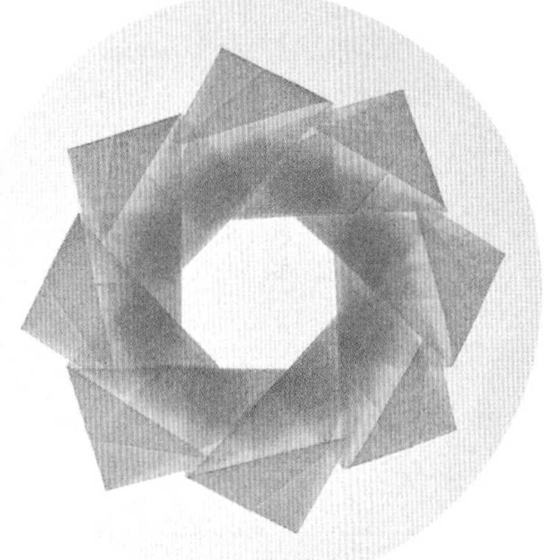

Ring 13-A　p68

Ring 25-B　p88

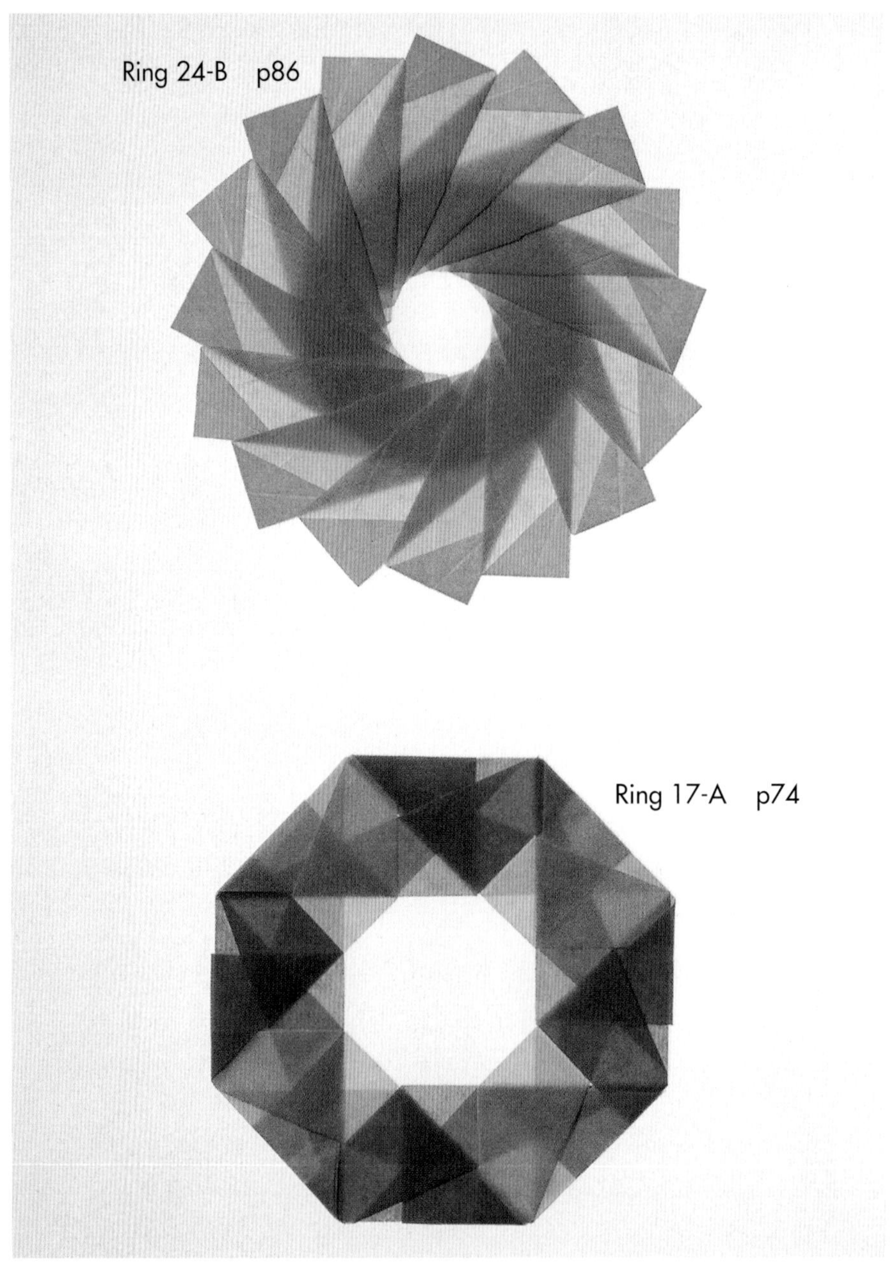


These rings are made of very thin paper. Light and shadow, and overlapping – these form new patterns.

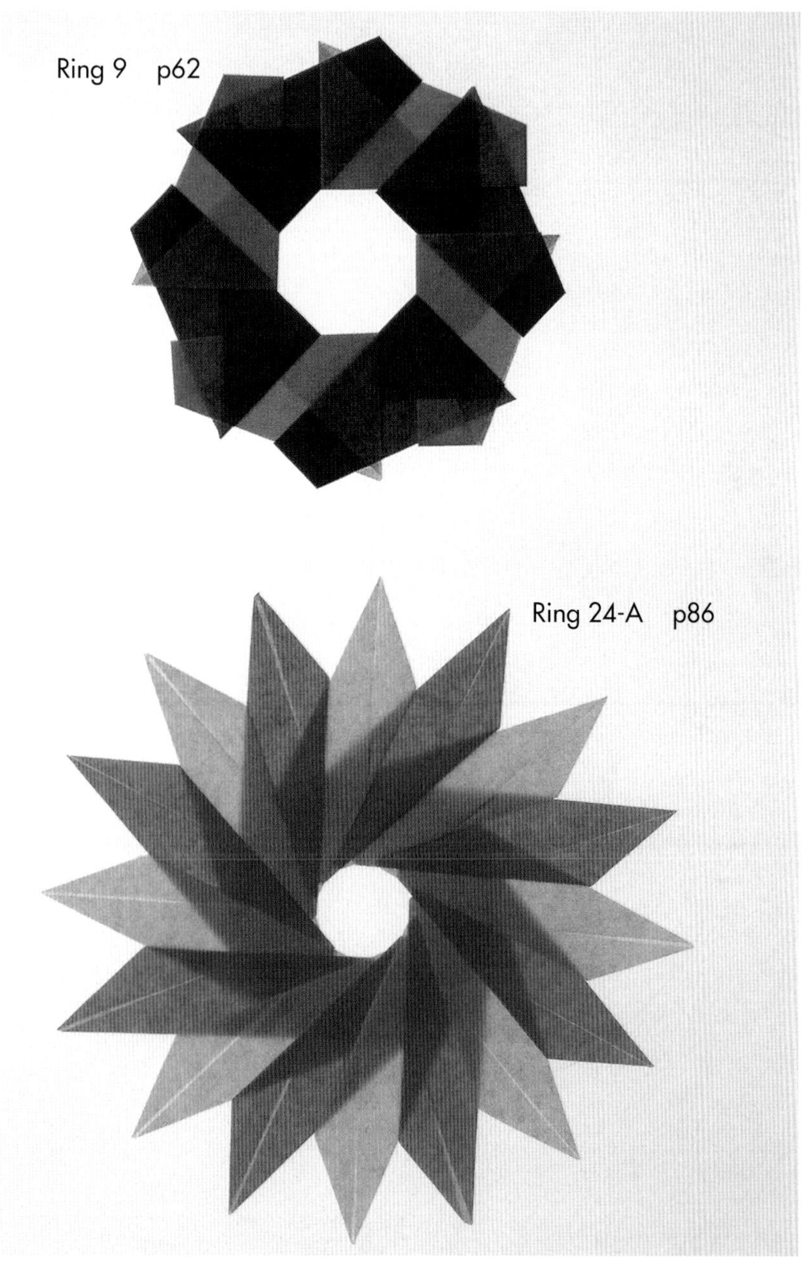
Ring 9 p62
Ring 24-A p86

I have arranged rings to make the Milky Way. These rings have already been introduced somewhere in the color pages. Can you find the pages? Try to look for them as if searching stars.

# Ring 19-A, B p77

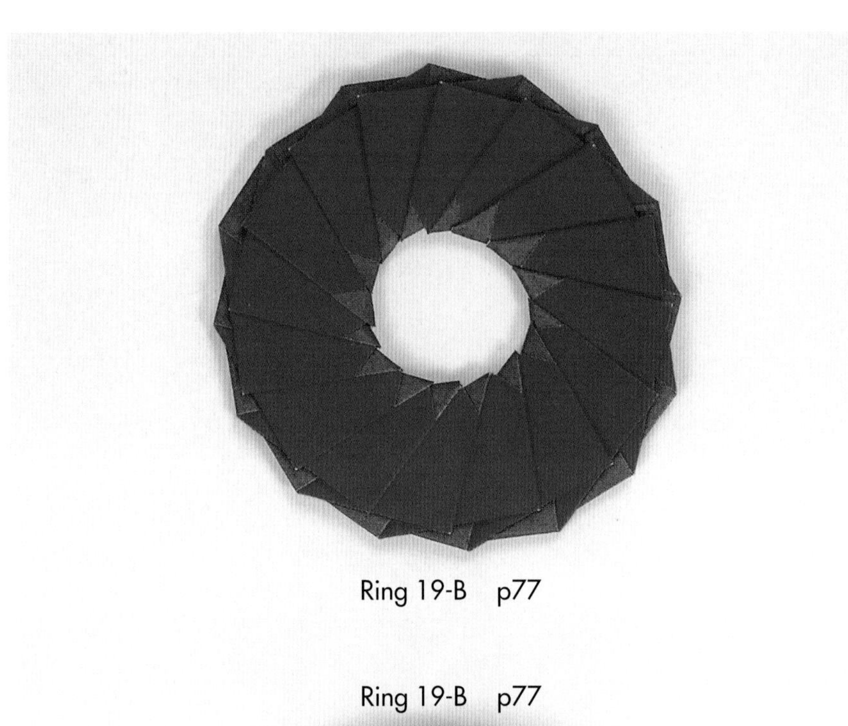

Ring 19-B p77

Ring 19-B p77

# The back of the rings on the left page

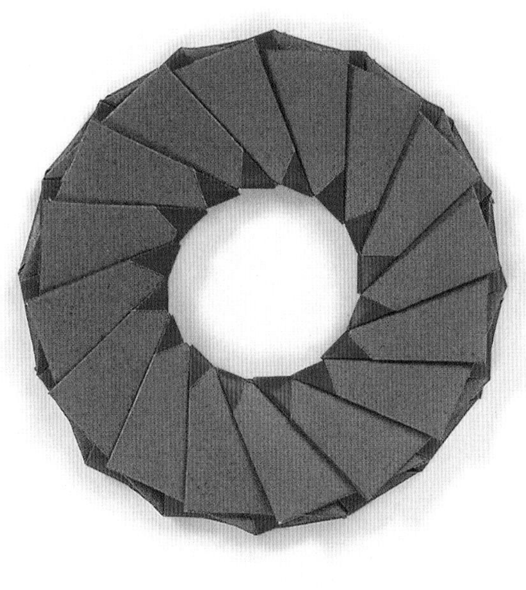

These are the back sides of the rings on the left page.
The color and patterns change dramatically.

# Ring 20-B, C, A p79

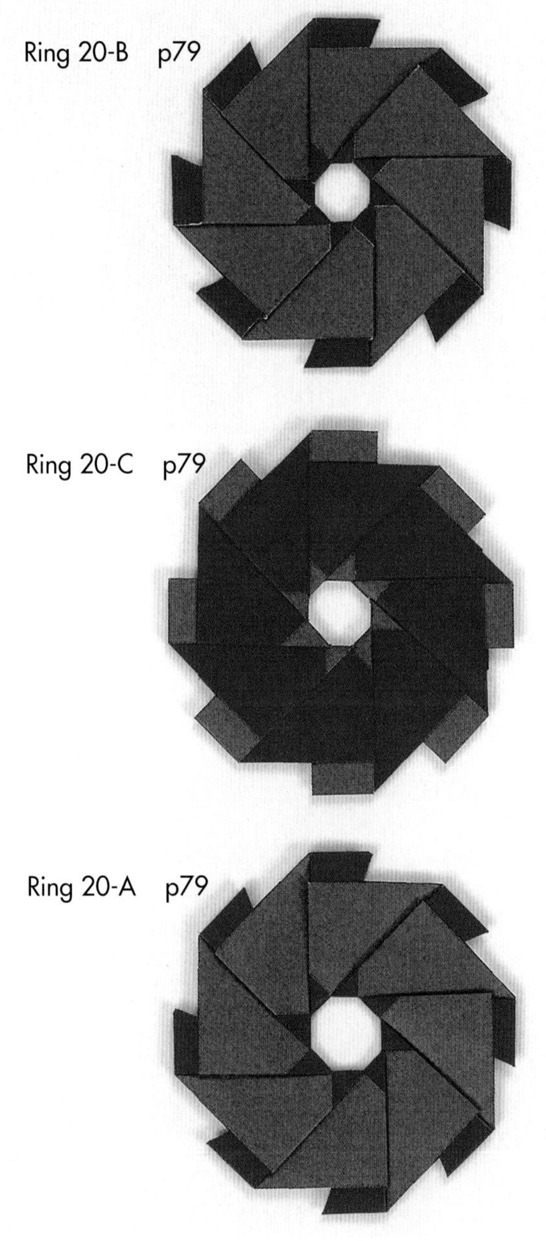
Ring 20-B p79

Ring 20-C p79

Ring 20-A p79

These are the back sides of the rings on the left page.
They look like magic tricks.

# Ring 23-12 units, 20 units p84

Ring 23-12units p84

Ring 23-20units p84

These are the back sides of the rings on the left page.
You cannot tell which is front and which is back.

Ring 22 p82 | 21-B p80
7-C p58 | 15 p71
9 p62

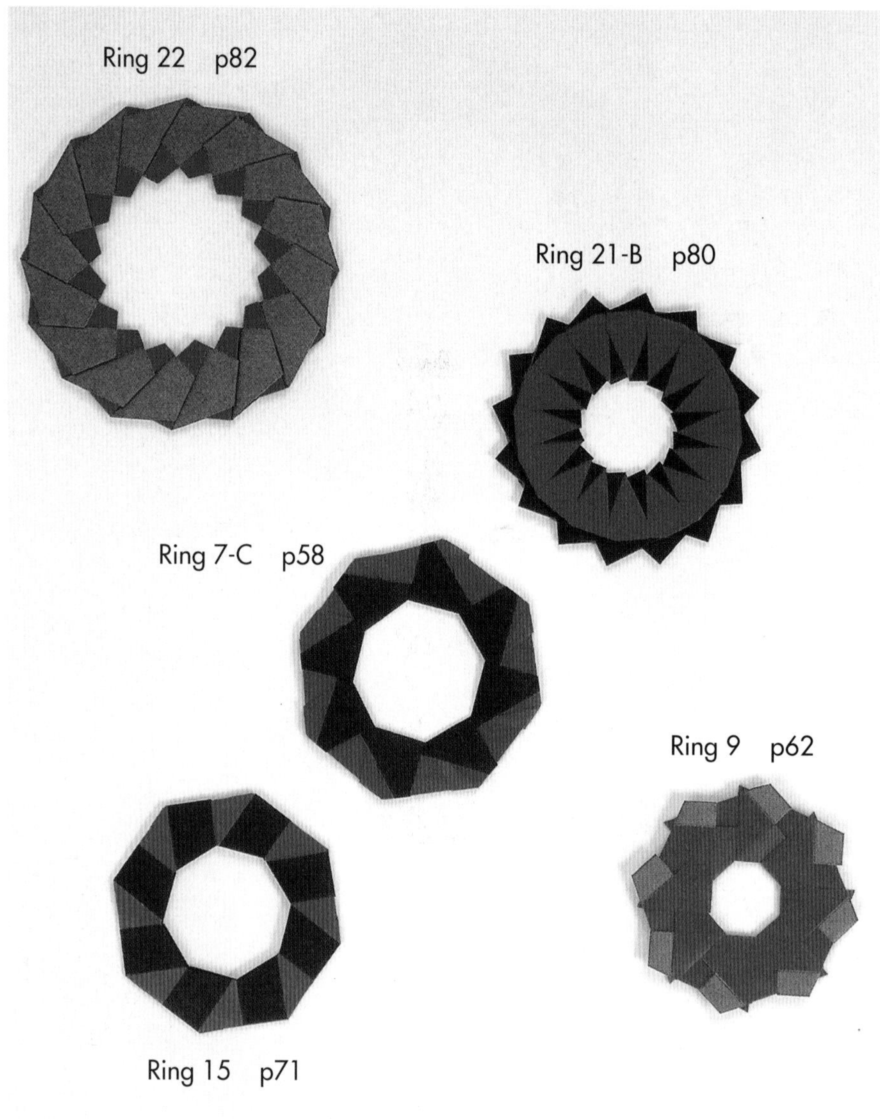

These are the back sides of the rings on the left page.
The joy is doubled.

Ring 23-16 units p84
15 p71
7-A p58

Ring 23-16units p84

Ring 15 p71

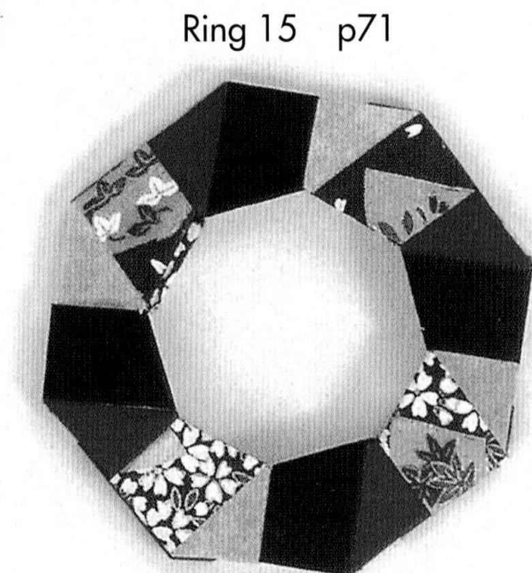

Ring 7-A p58

I have used Japanese paper which is lined on both sides.
The thickness and weight is the feature of the exquisite texture.
It is not just seeing but the feeling to touch that gives us the pleasure of origami.

Ring 27 p91

Ring 27 p91

Ring 23-20units p84

# Ring 24-A, B p86
# 25-B, A p88

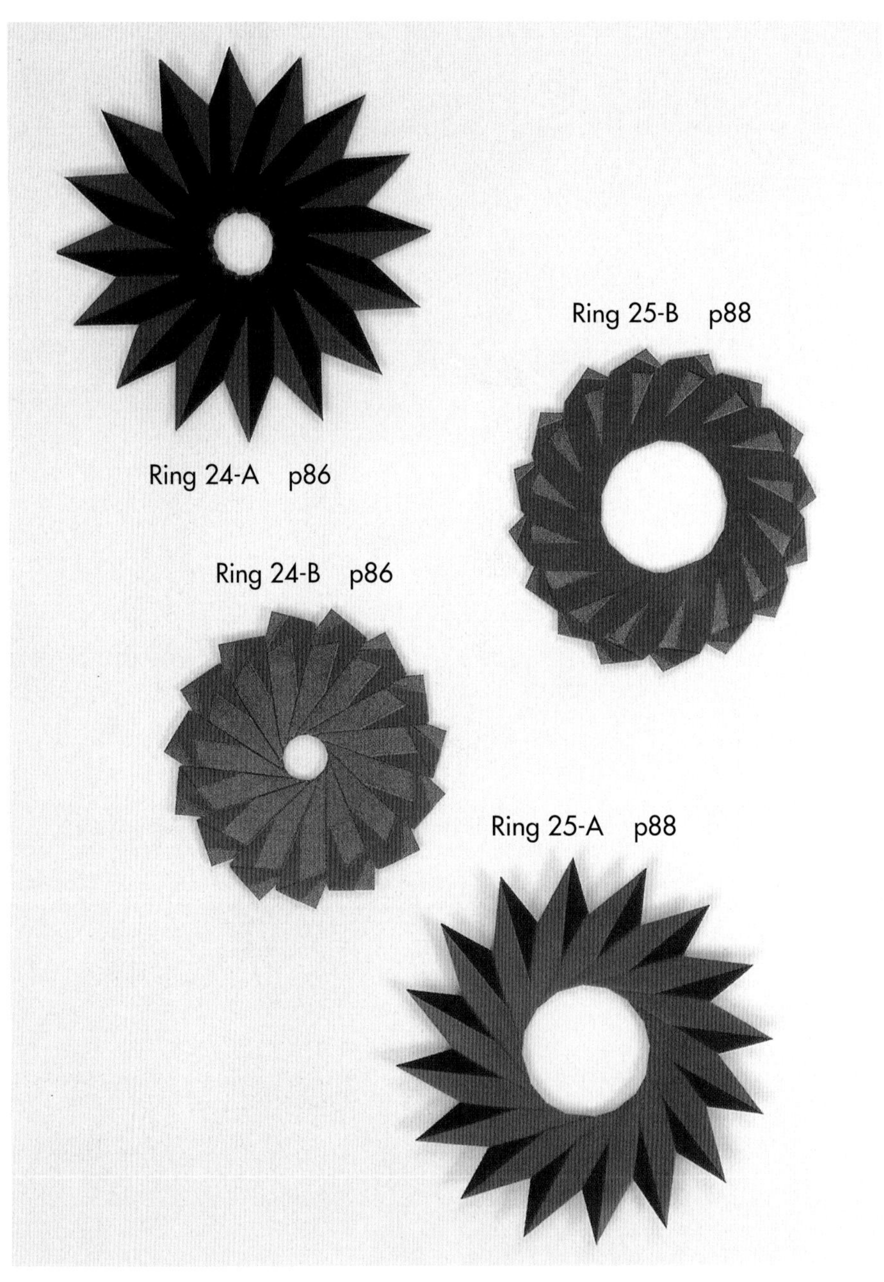


If you fold the pointed tips, you can make different rings.

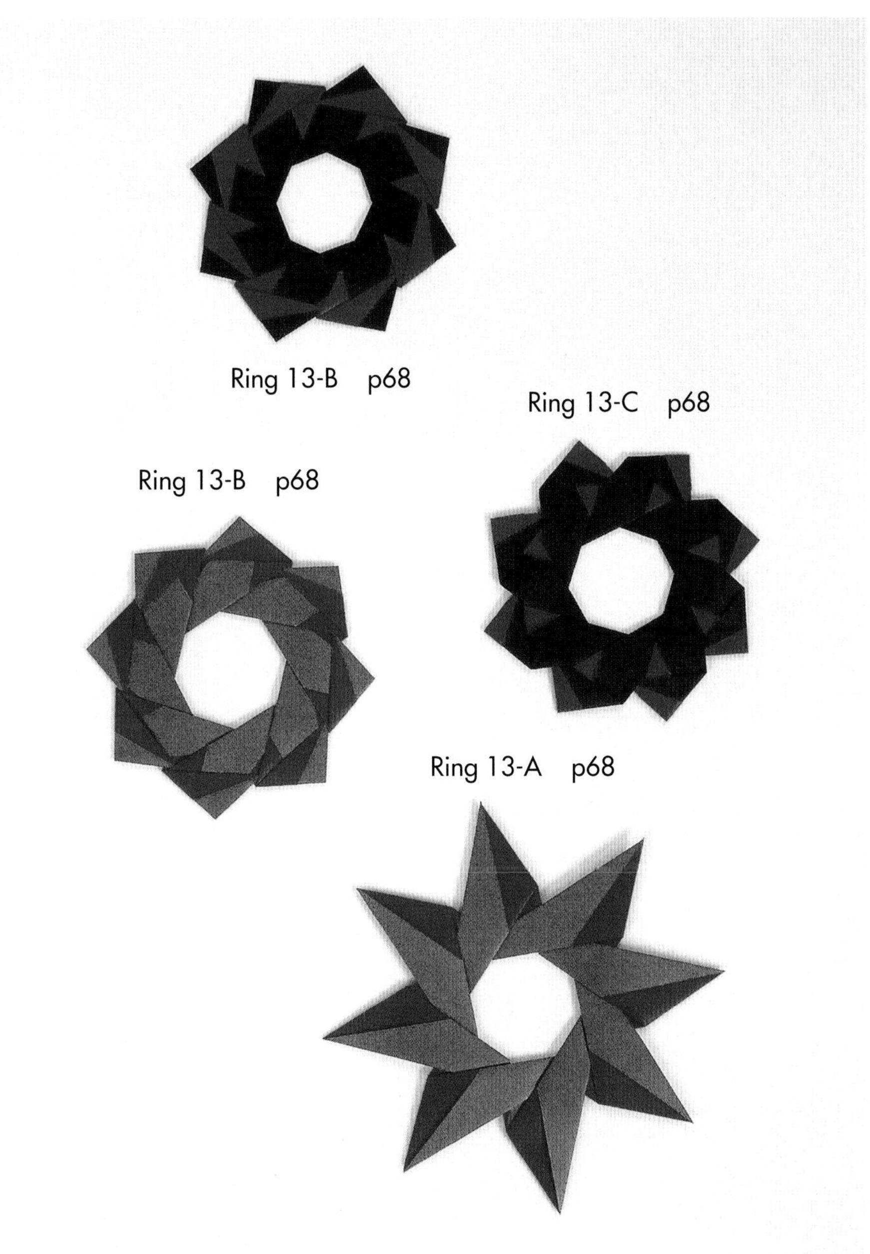

Ring 13-B p68

Ring 13-C p68

Ring 13-B p68

Ring 13-A p68

In which directions will you fold the pointed tips of the basic stars? You may fold as you desire.

# A variety of rings

I have put the rings on stands.
Do they look like the flowers in the flower garden, or loops used in the circus? The rings appeared once somewhere in this color pages.

# Ring 10 p63

This thick, heavy and gorgeous ring is made of paper with golden and silver marbling patterns.

# Symbols and Folding Techniques

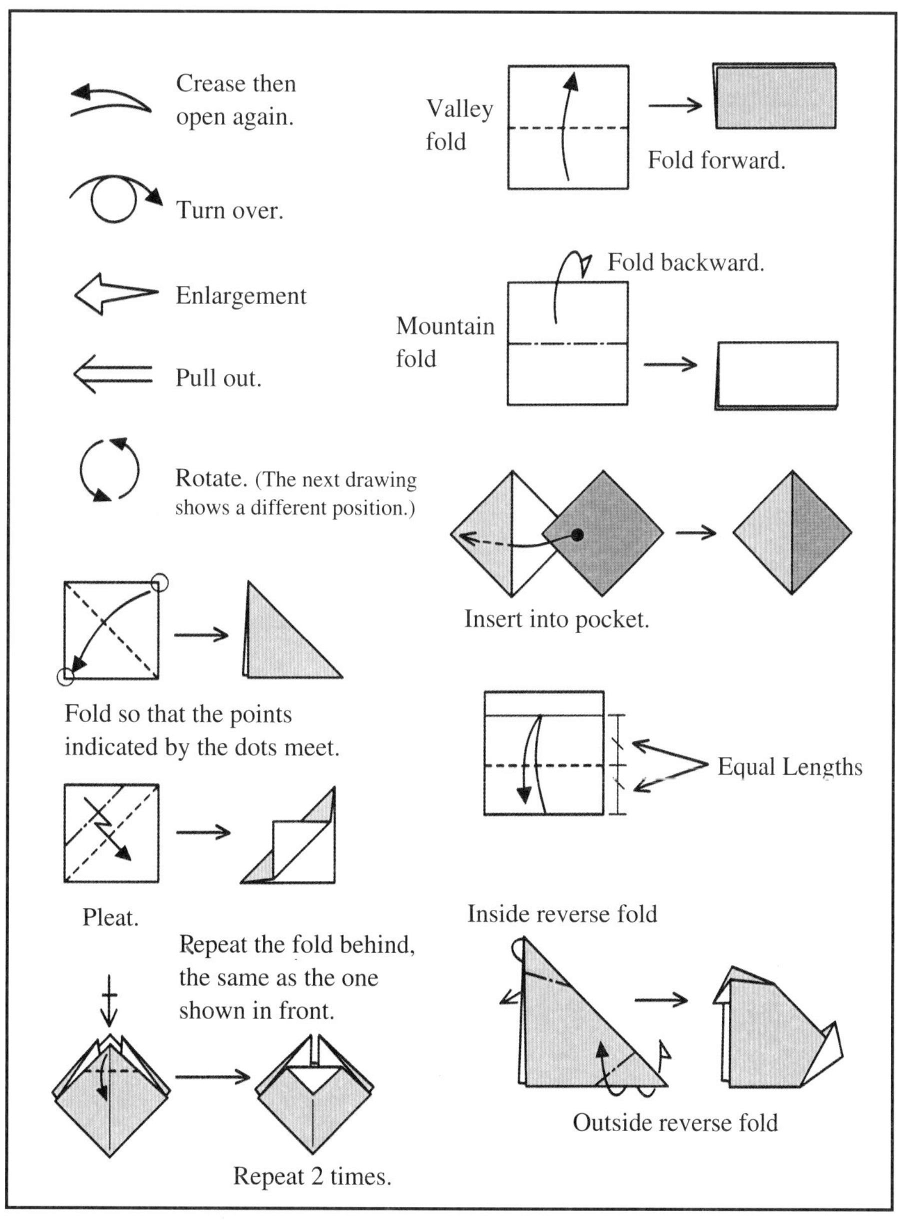

# RING 1

Standard paper size:
7.5cm×7.5cm (3 in×3 in)

Joined firmly by eight units.
The front and back sides have the same patterns.

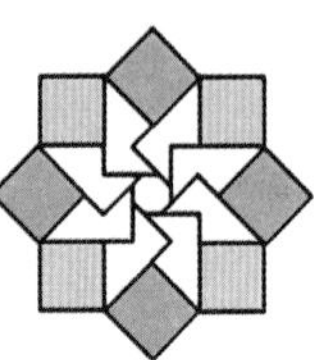

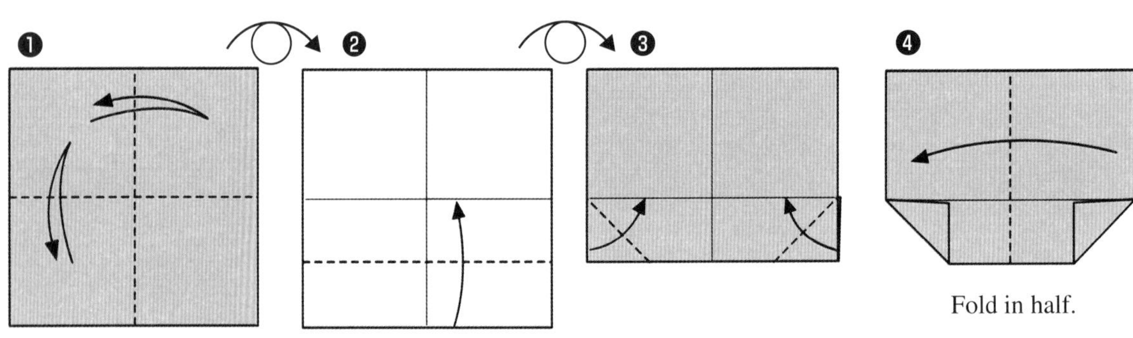

Fold in half.

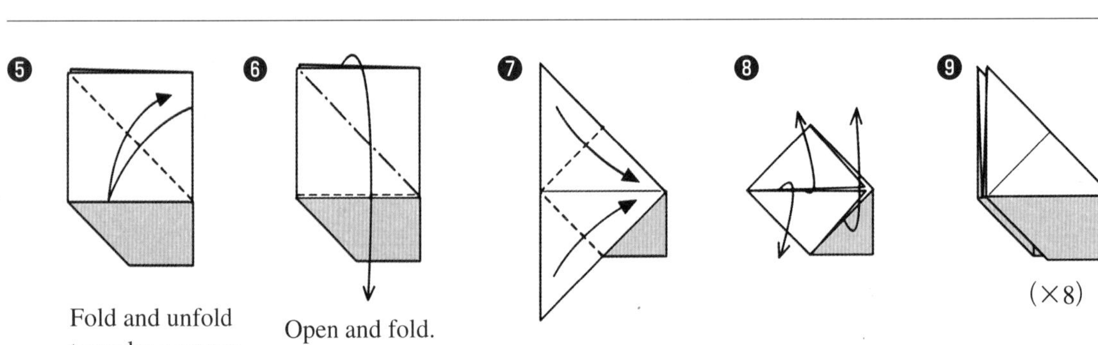

Fold and unfold to make a crease.

Open and fold.

(×8)

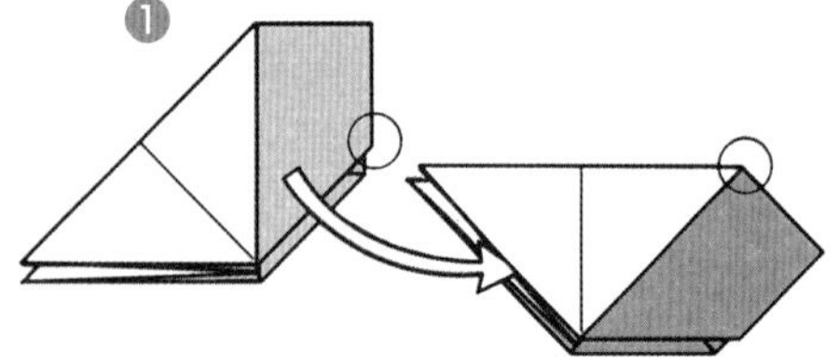

Insert so that the circles ◯ meet.

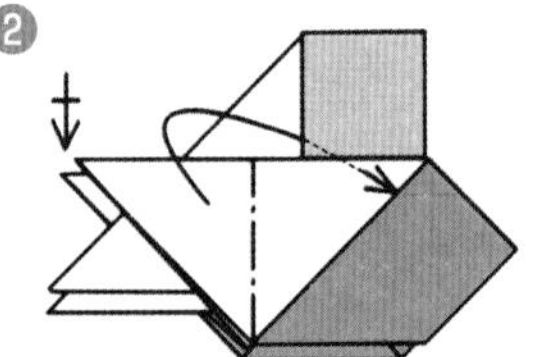

Turn back and insert into the back pocket. Fold the other side in the same way.

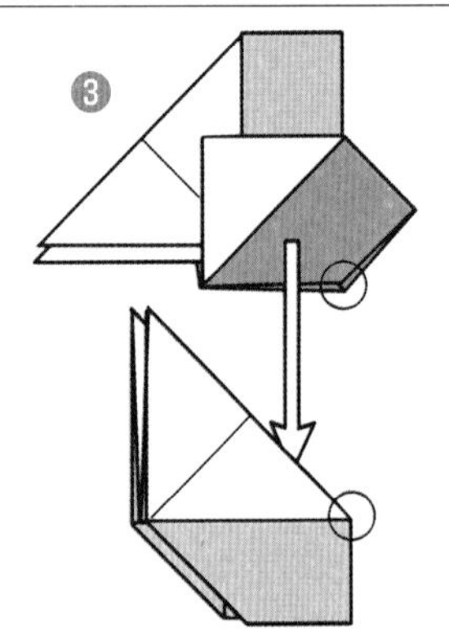

Insert so that the circles ◯ meet.

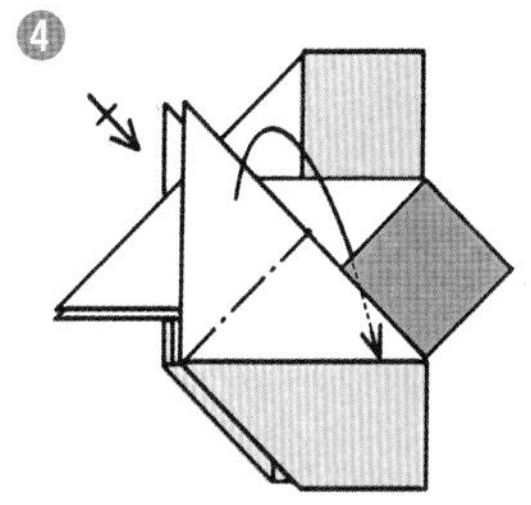

Turn back and insert into the back pocket. Fold the other side in the same way.

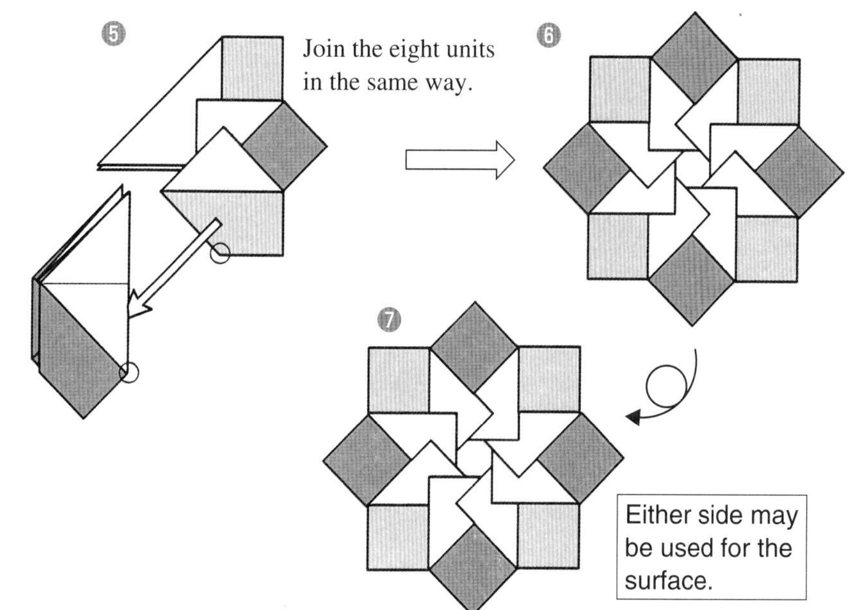

Join the eight units in the same way.

Either side may be used for the surface.

# RING 2

Standard paper size:
7.5cm×7.5cm (3 in×3 in)

Joined firmly by means of three locks.
The front and back sides have different patterns.

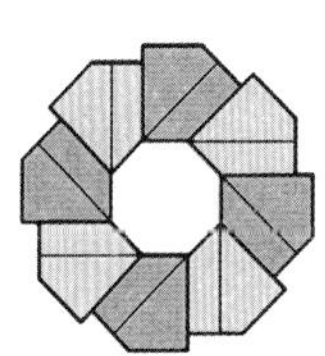

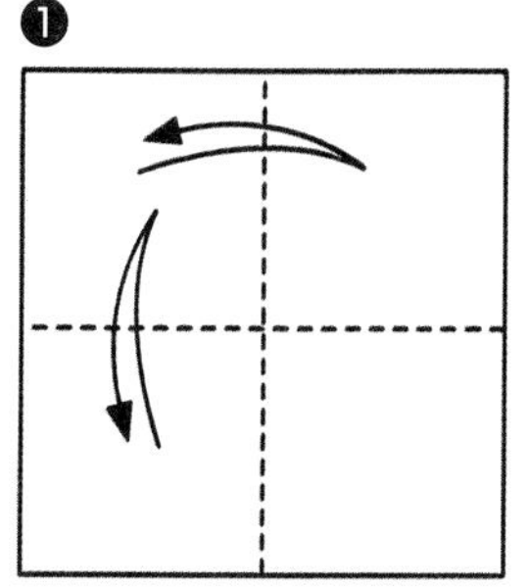

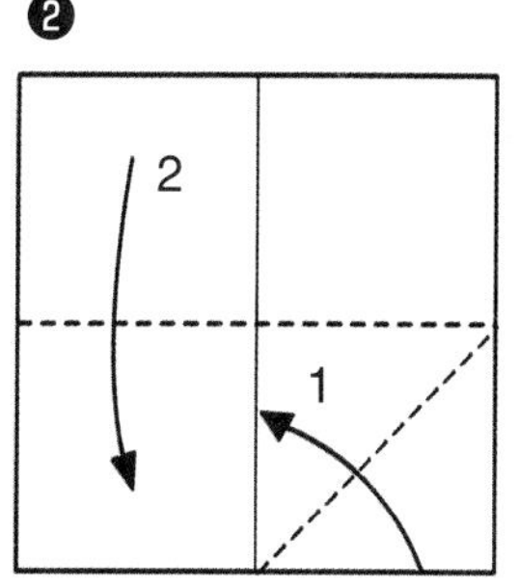


Fold in numerical order.

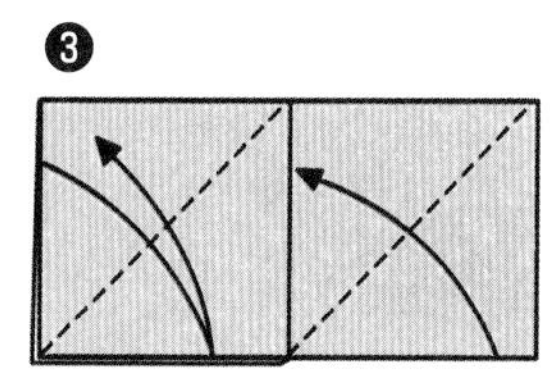

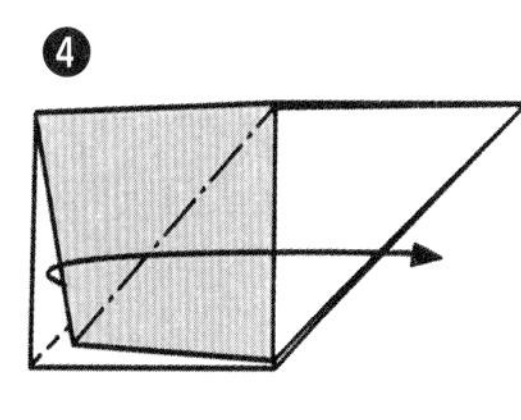

Open.

Continued on the next page.

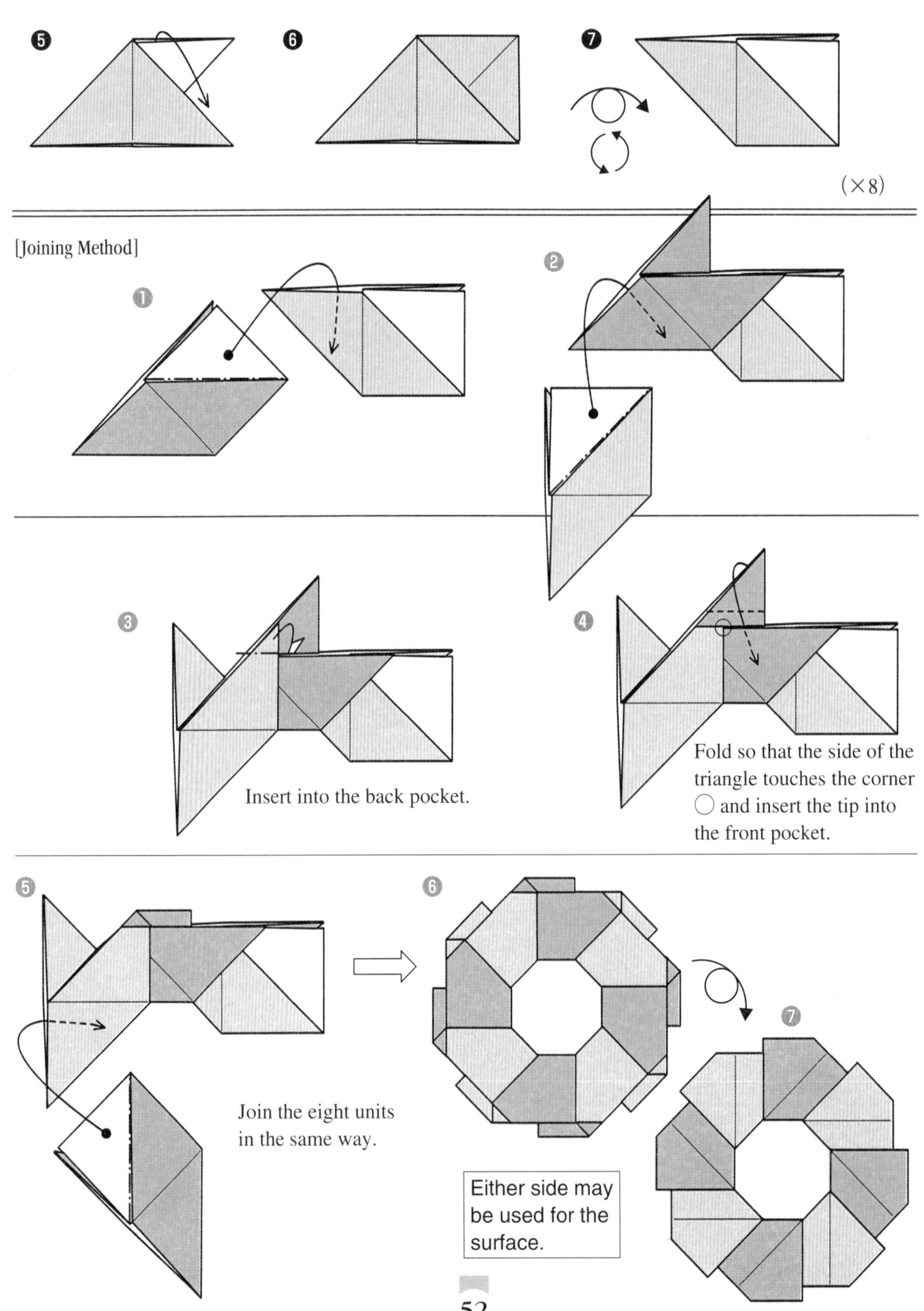

5
6
7
(×8)
[Joining Method]
1
2
3
Insert into the back pocket.
4
Fold so that the side of the triangle touches the corner ◯ and insert the tip into the front pocket.
5
Join the eight units in the same way.
6
Either side may be used for the surface.
7

# RING 3

**Standard paper size:**
**7.5cm×7.5cm (3 in×3 in)**

Closely related with Ring 2. Joined by means of two locks.
The front and back sides have different patterns.

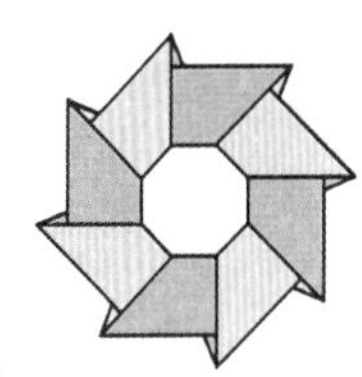

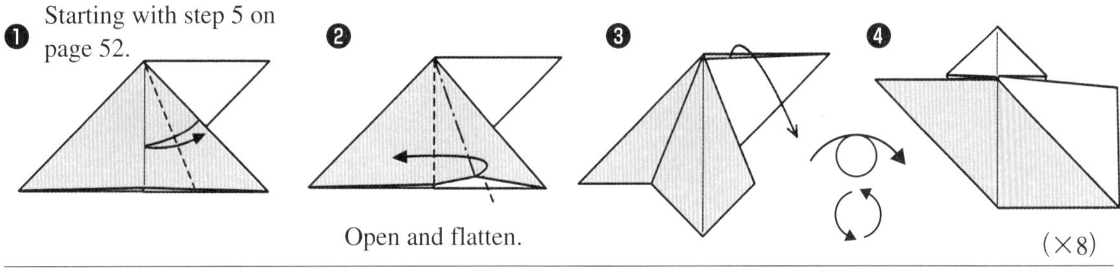


[Joining Method]

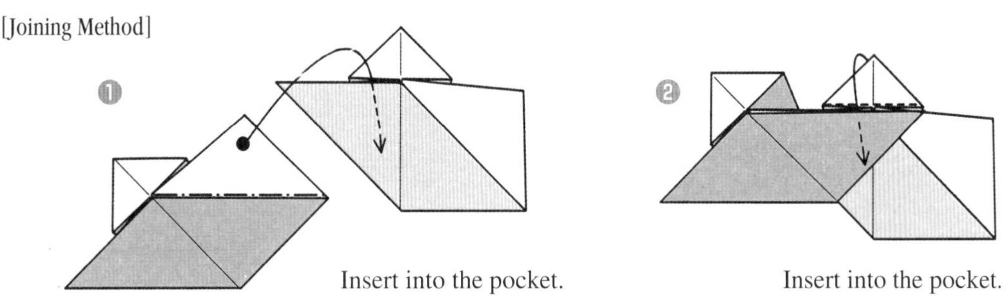


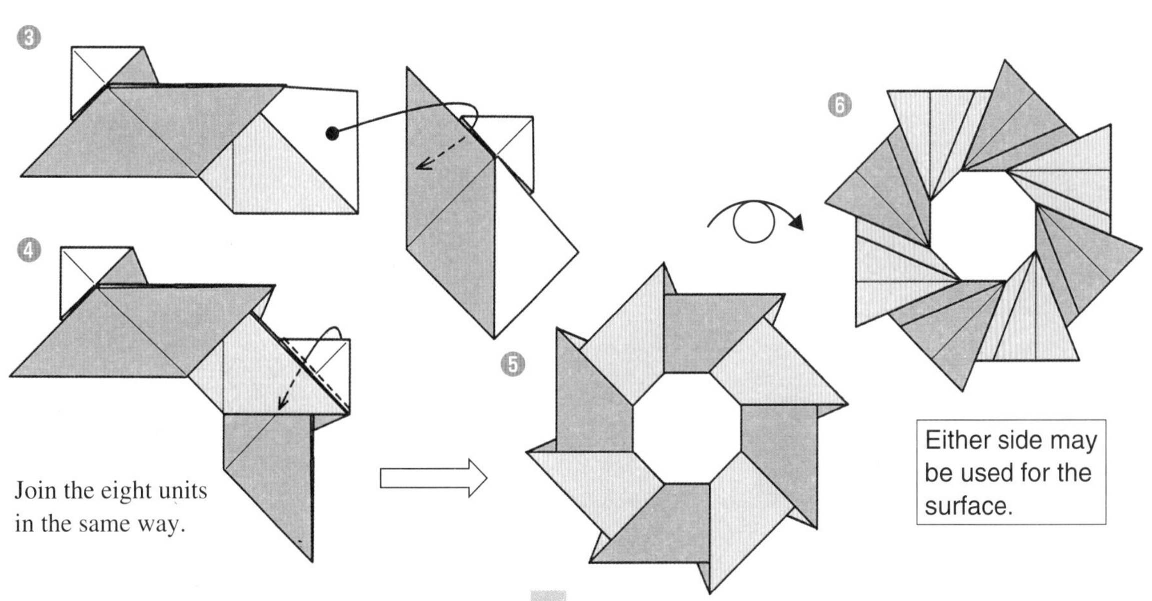

# RING 4

**Standard paper size:**
**7.5cm×7.5cm (3 in×3 in)**

This is almost the same as Ring 2, but the back side is first made.

1

2

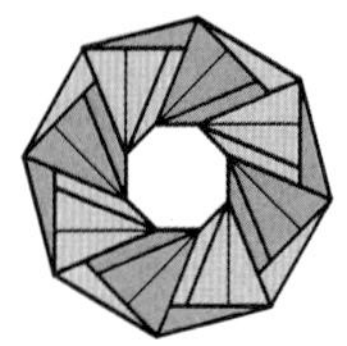

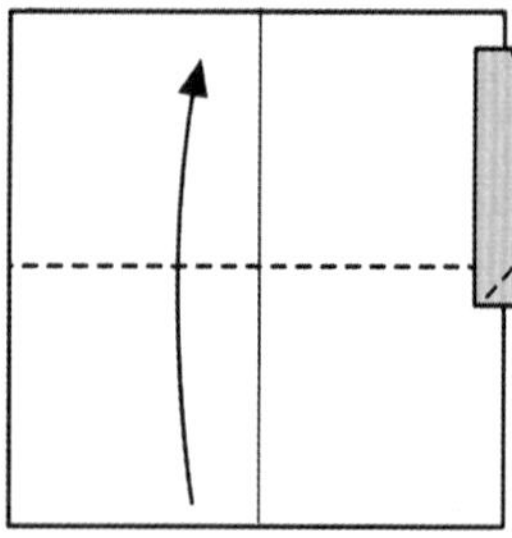

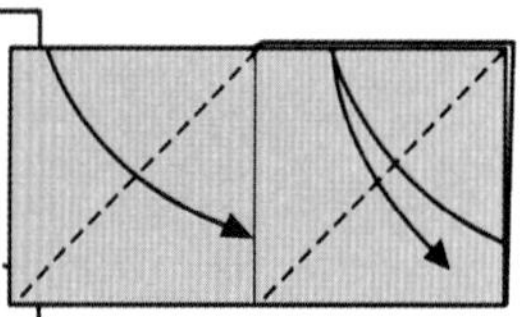

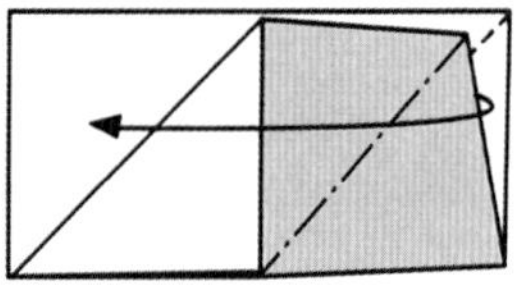

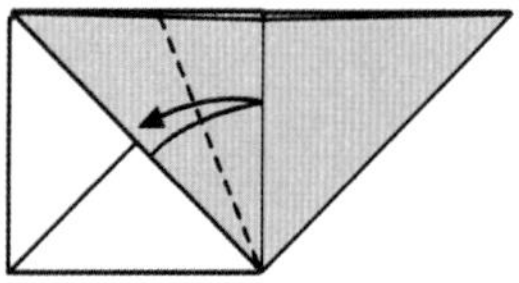

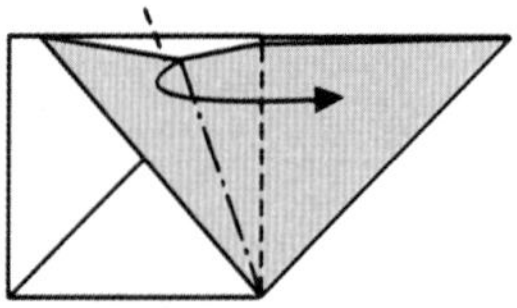

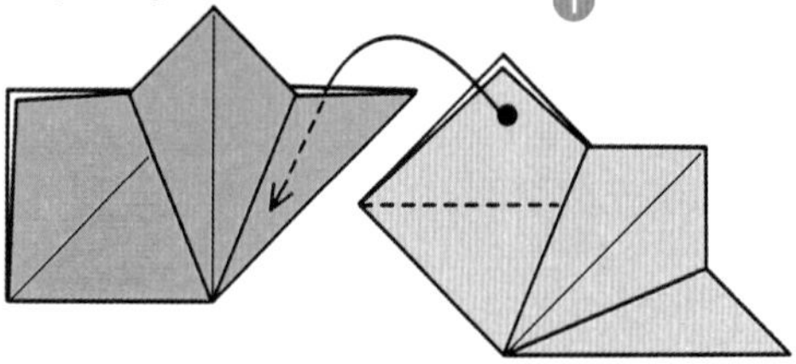

Fold only the upper left flap.

3

4

5

6

(×8)

[Joining Method]

1

2

Insert into the back pocket.

3

It will be better to fold flap (a) after all the units were joined.

4

Join the eight units in the same way.

5

6

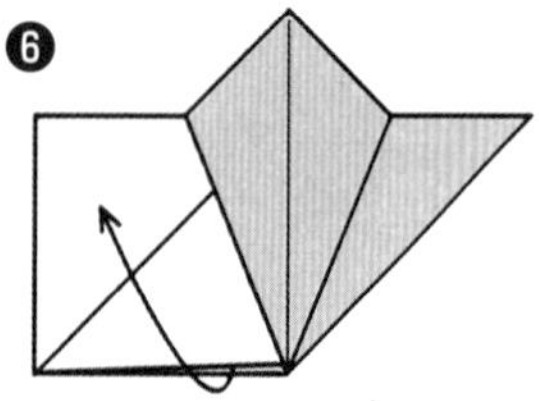

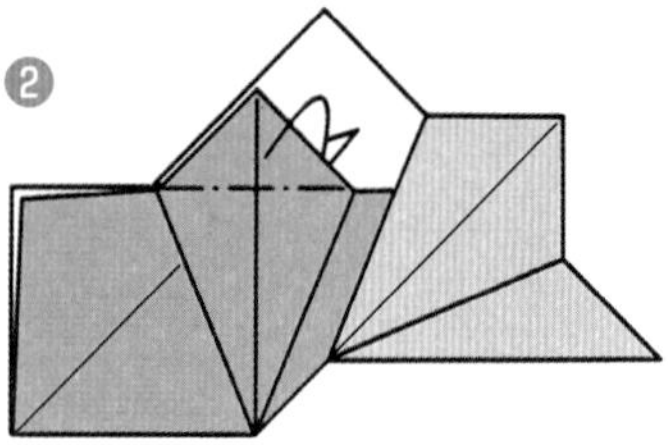

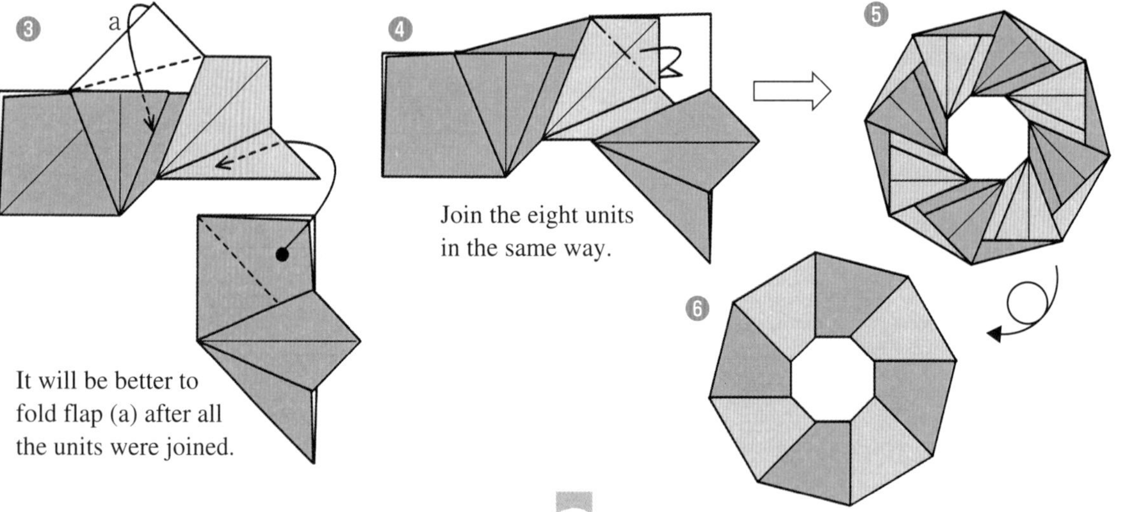

# RING 5

Standard paper size:
7.5cm×7.5cm (3 in×3 in)

A ring with eight horns. The front and back sides have the same patterns.

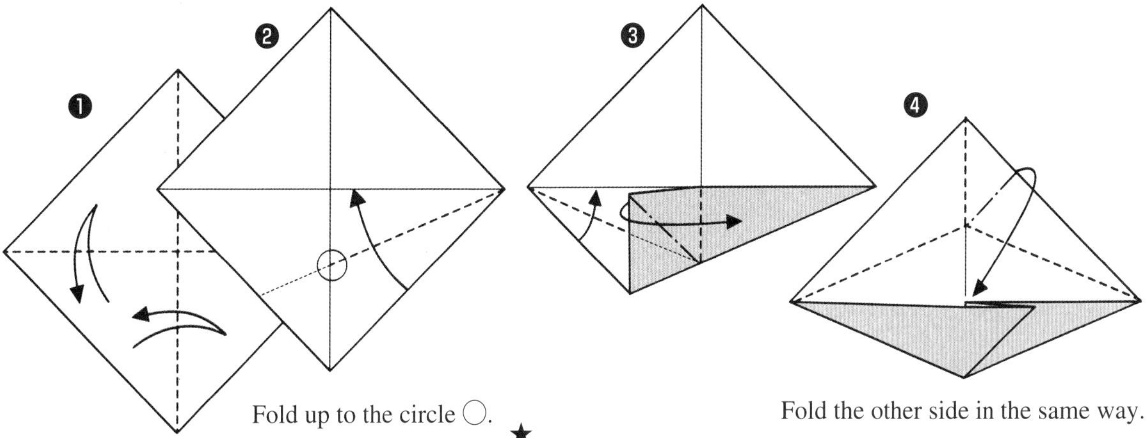

❶ ❷ ❸ ❹

Fold up to the circle ◯.

Fold the other side in the same way.

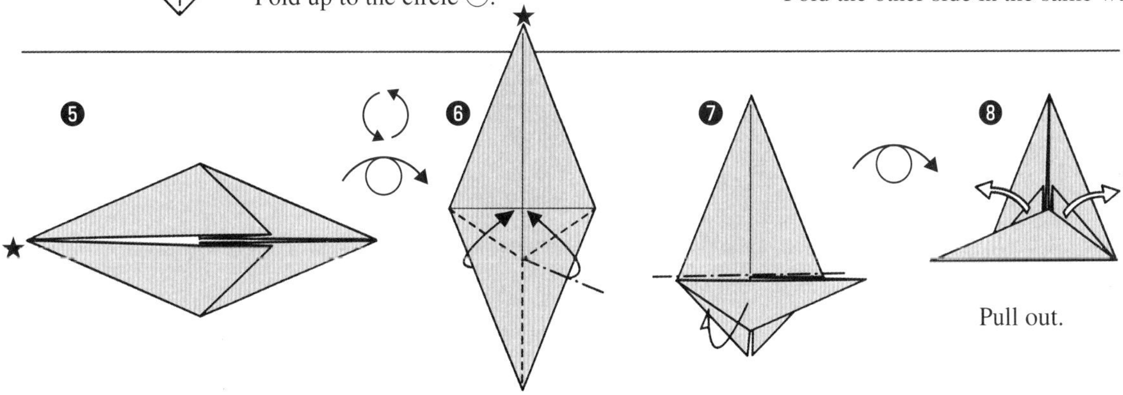

❺ ❻ ❼ ❽

Pull out.

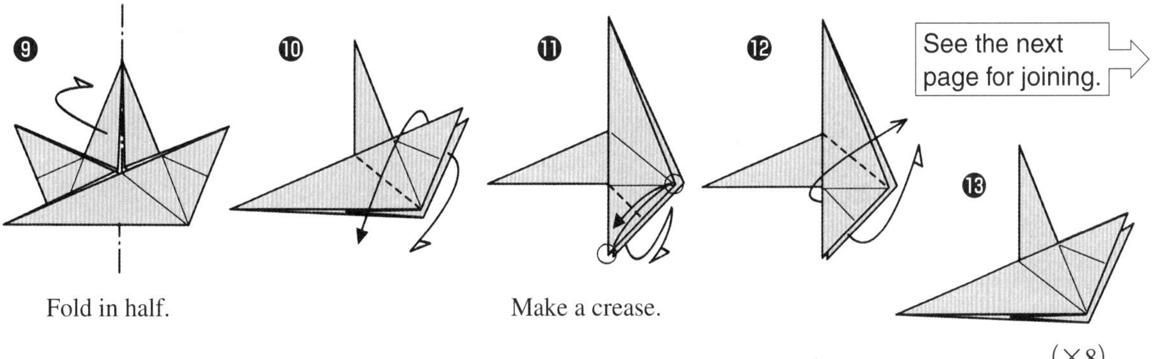

❾ ❿ ⓫ ⓬ ⓭

Fold in half.

Make a crease.

See the next page for joining.

(×8)

[Joining Method]

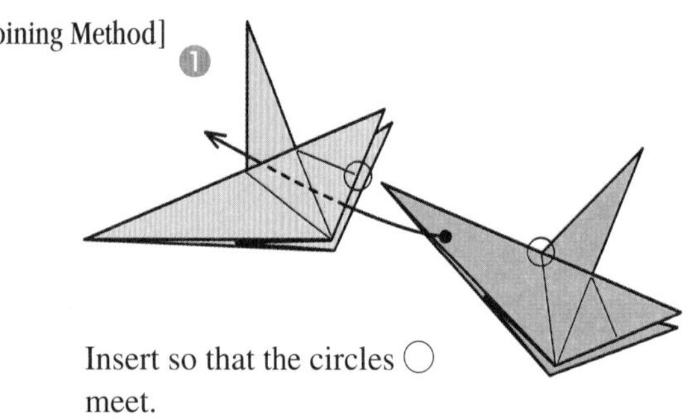


Insert so that the circles ◯ meet.

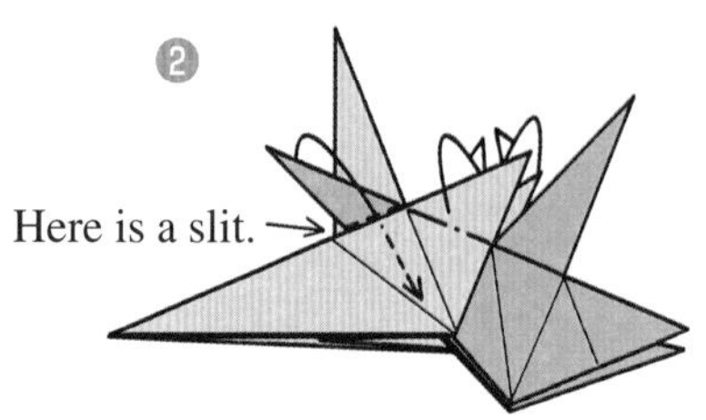


Tuck both triangles into the slit.

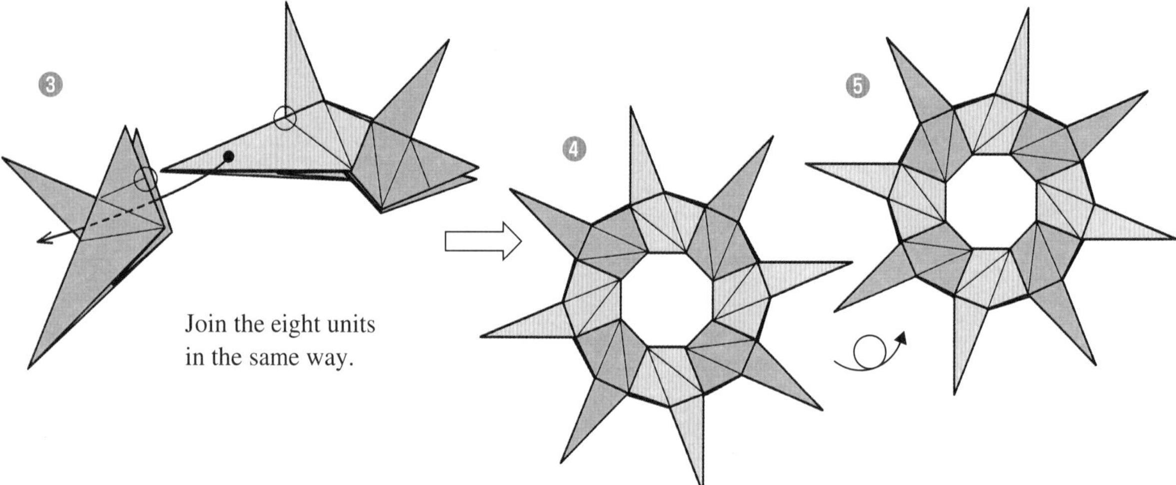


Join the eight units in the same way.

# RING 6

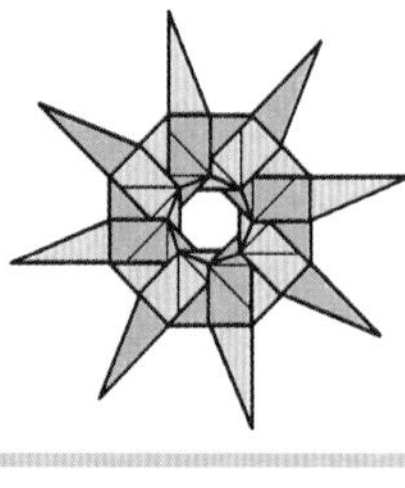

Standard paper size:
7.5cm×7.5cm (3in×3in)

The folding method is basically the same as that of Ring 5.
The only difference is how to make the horns.

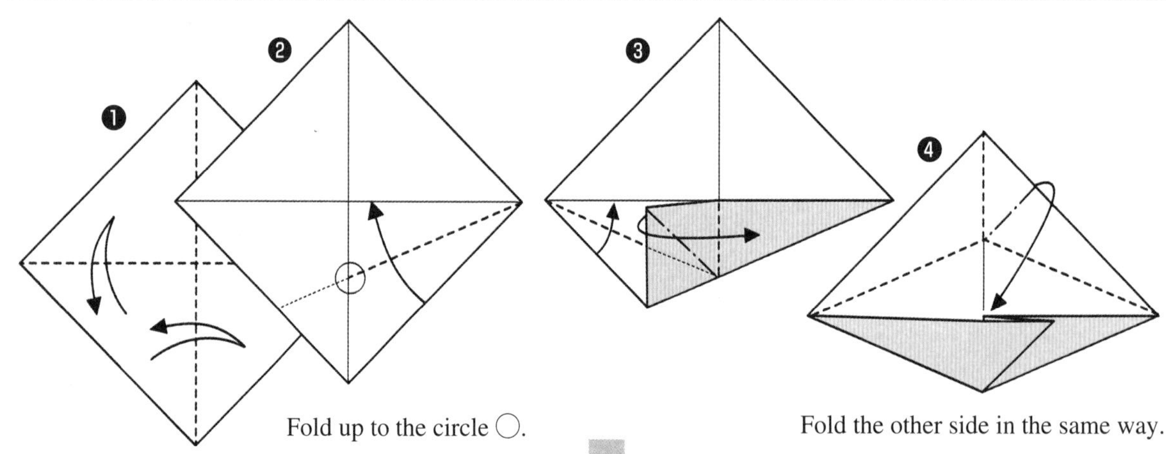


Fold up to the circle ◯.

Fold the other side in the same way.

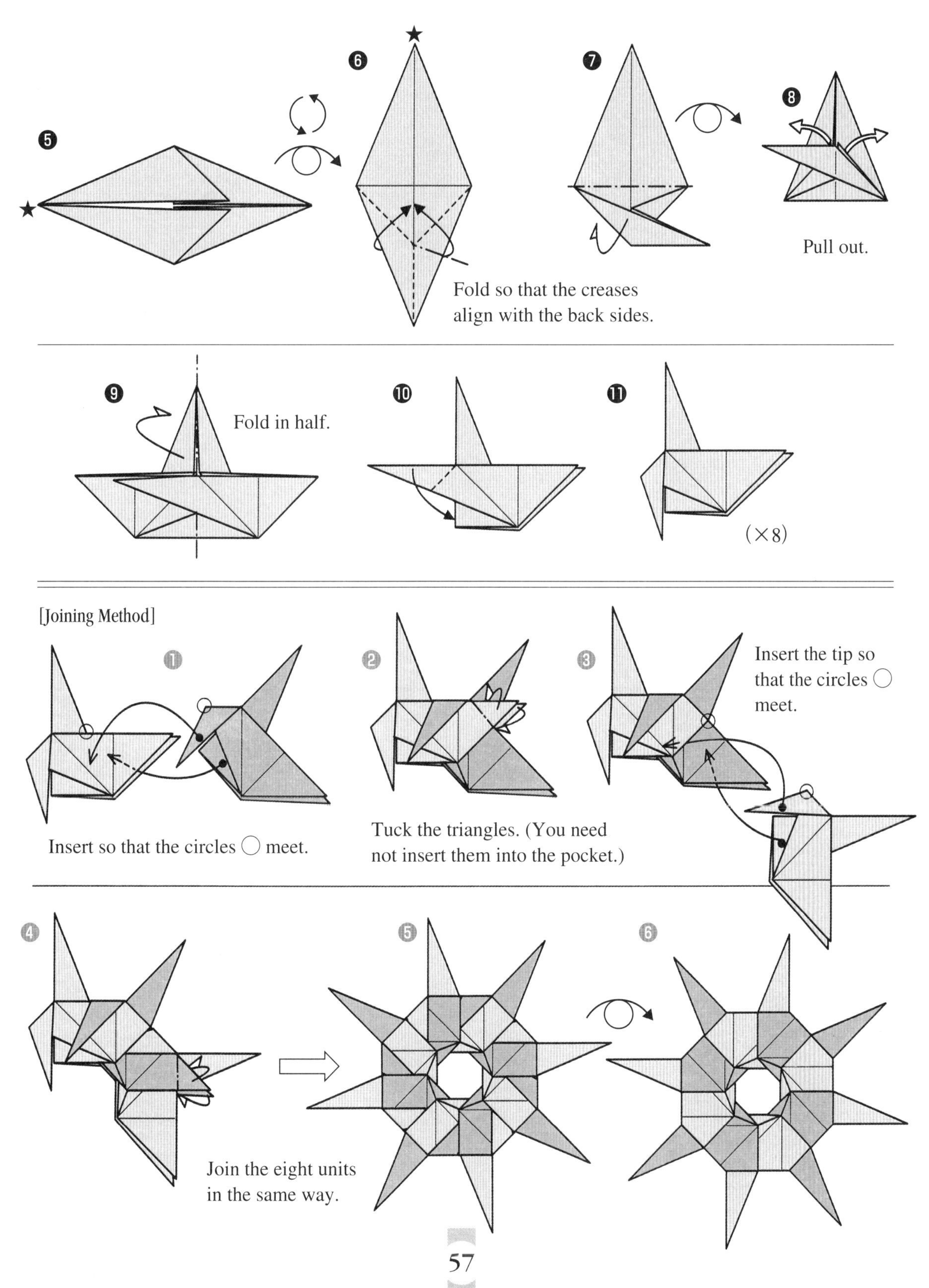
5
6
7
8
Pull out.
Fold so that the creases
align with the back sides.
9
Fold in half.
10
11
(×8)
[Joining Method]
1
Insert so that the circles ◯ meet.
2
Tuck the triangles. (You need
not insert them into the pocket.)
3
Insert the tip so
that the circles ◯
meet.
4
Join the eight units
in the same way.
5
6

# RING 7

Standard paper size:
7.5cm×7.5cm (3 in×3 in)

A little change in folding produces variations in color.
Try to join units of different colors.

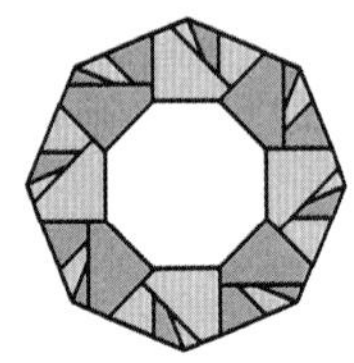

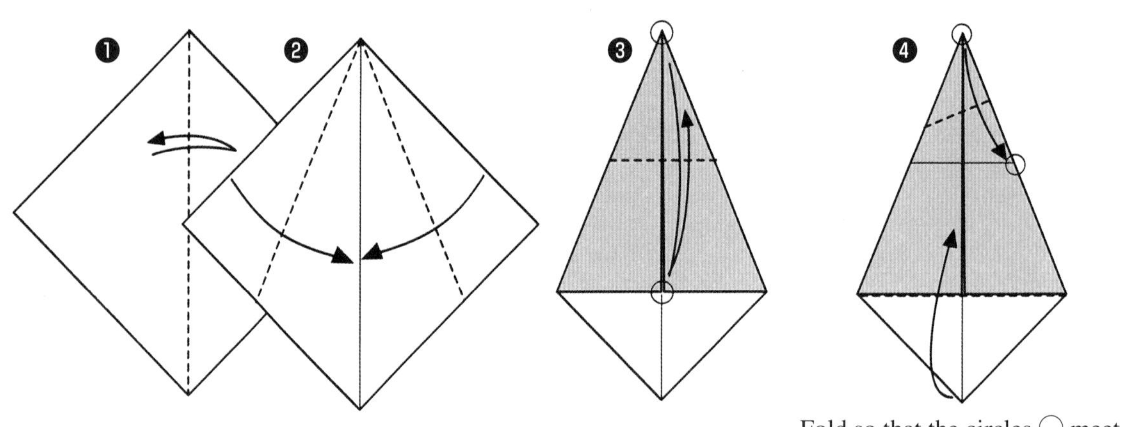

❶ ❷ ❸ ❹

Fold so that the circles ◯ meet.

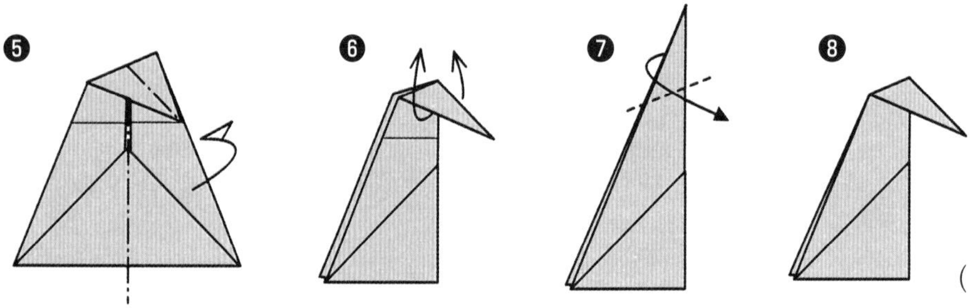

❺ Fold in half.

❻ Unfold the triangle.

❼ Fold together towards you.

❽ (×8)

[Joining Method]

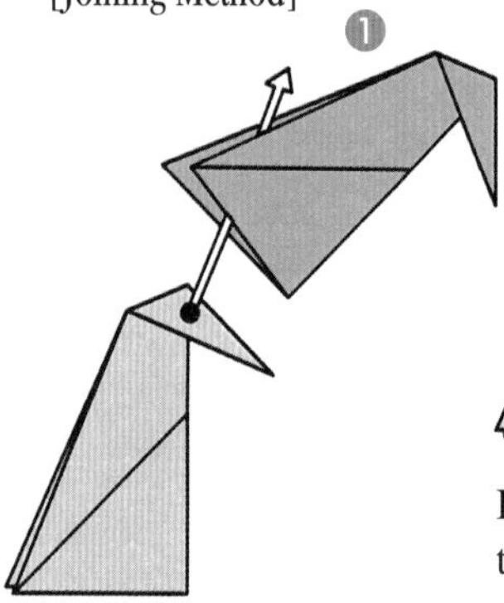

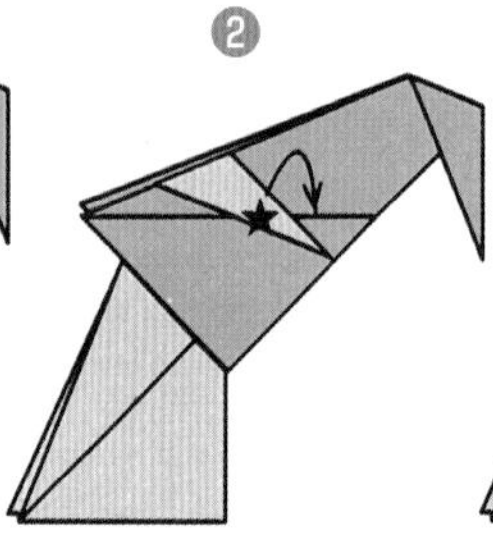

❶

❷ Insert the tip ★ into the pocket.

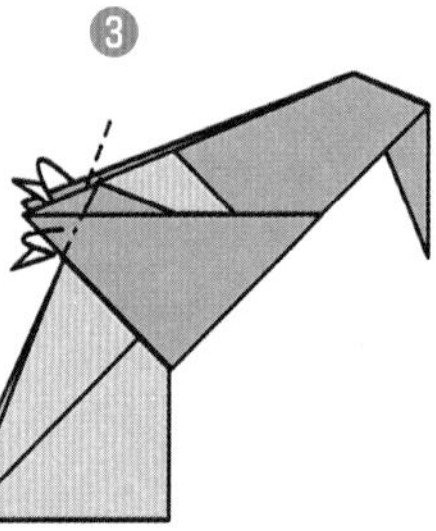

❸ Tuck inward.

❹

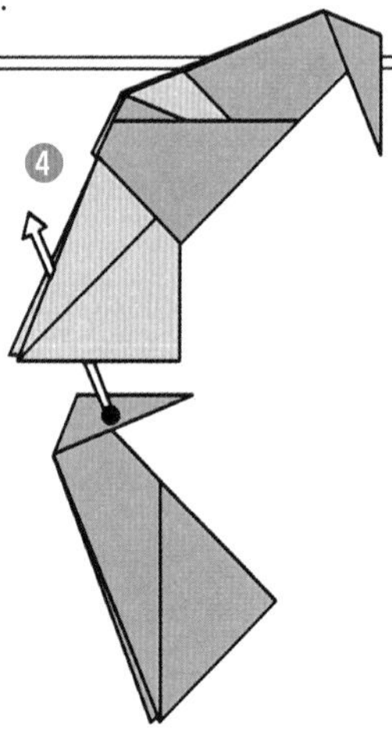

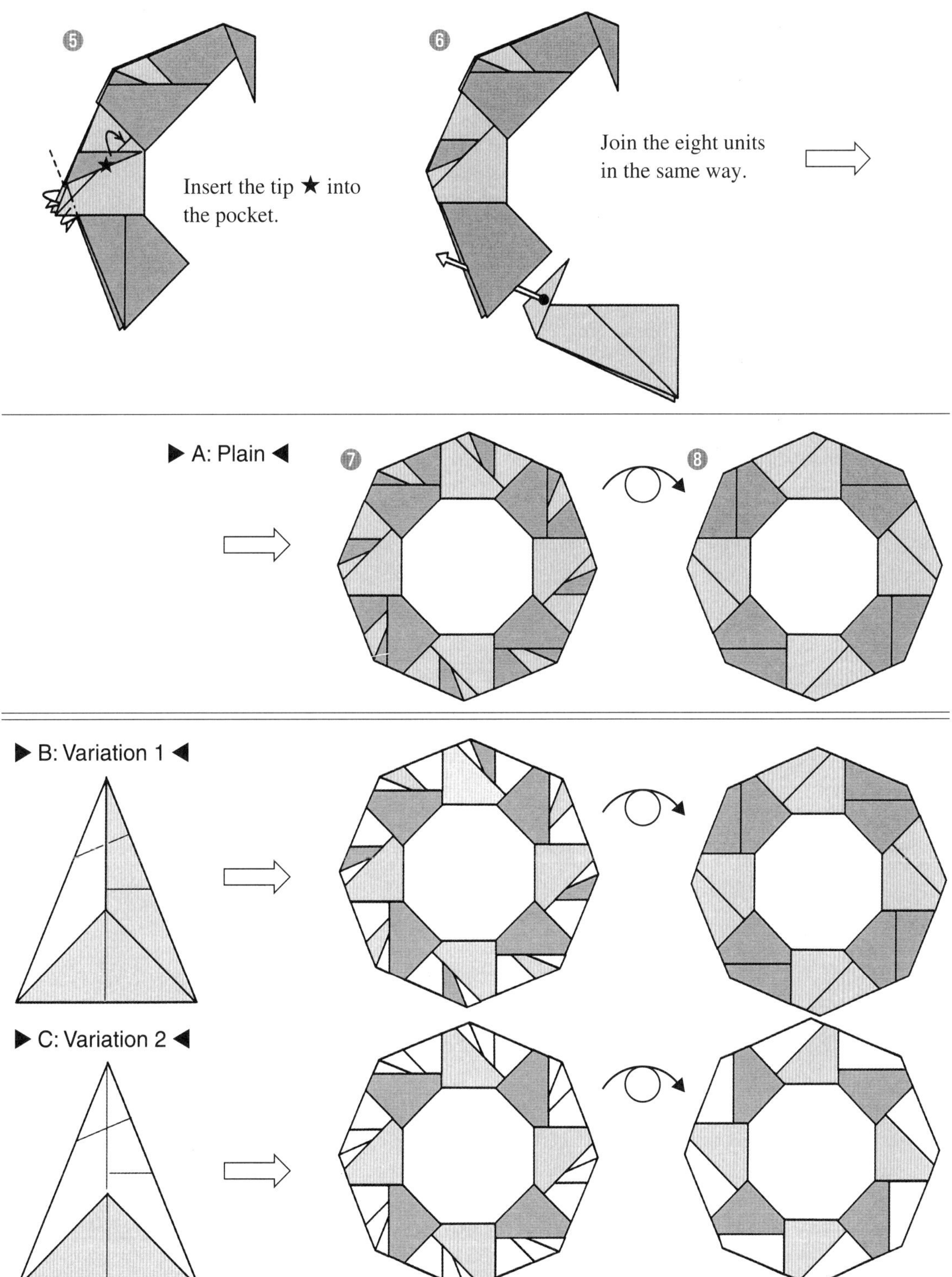
5
Insert the tip ★ into the pocket.
6
Join the eight units in the same way.
▶ A: Plain ◀
7
8
▶ B: Variation 1 ◀
▶ C: Variation 2 ◀

# RING 8

Standard paper size:
7.5cm×7.5cm (3 in×3 in)

This ring consists of 16 units. The last several units are joined up to ❸ and shape them up before inserting the tip into the pocket.

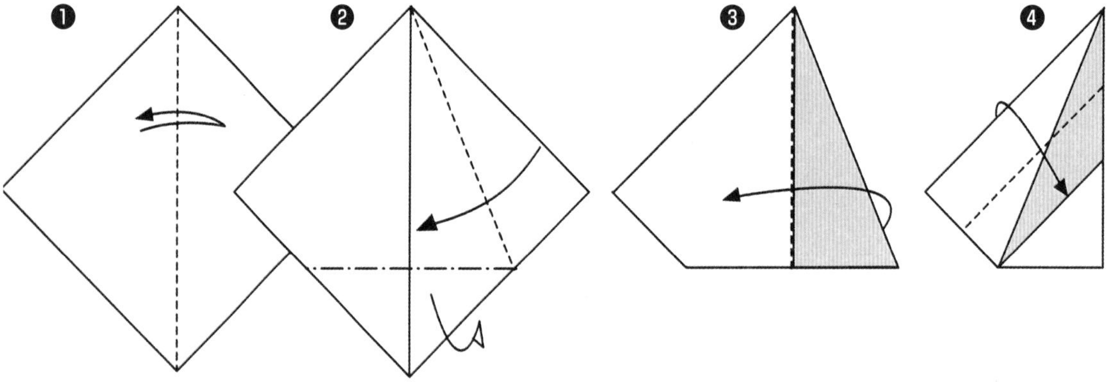

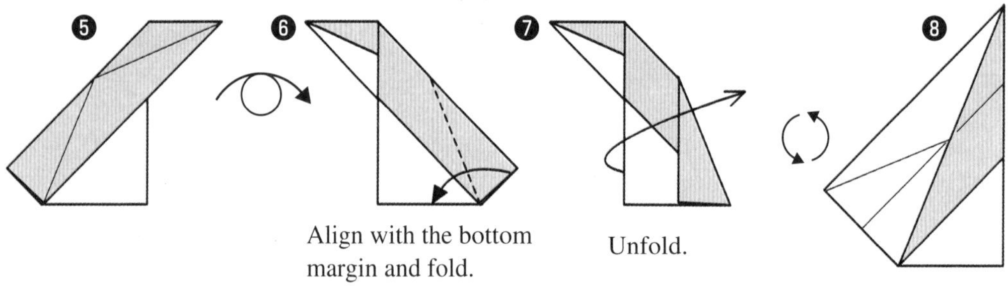

❶ ❷ ❸ ❹

❺ ❻ ❼ ❽

Align with the bottom margin and fold.

Unfold.

(×16)

[Joining Method]

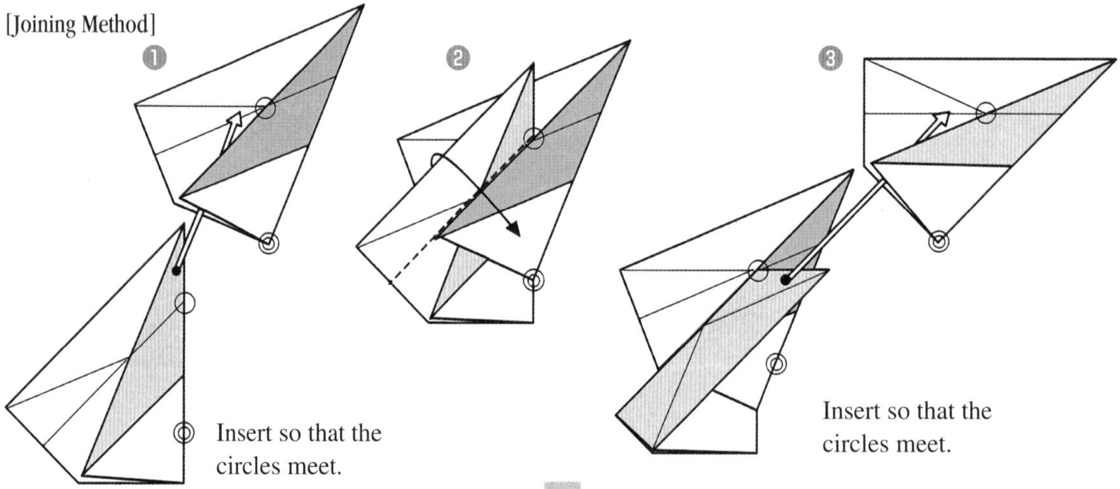

❶ ❷ ❸

Insert so that the circles meet.

Insert so that the circles meet.

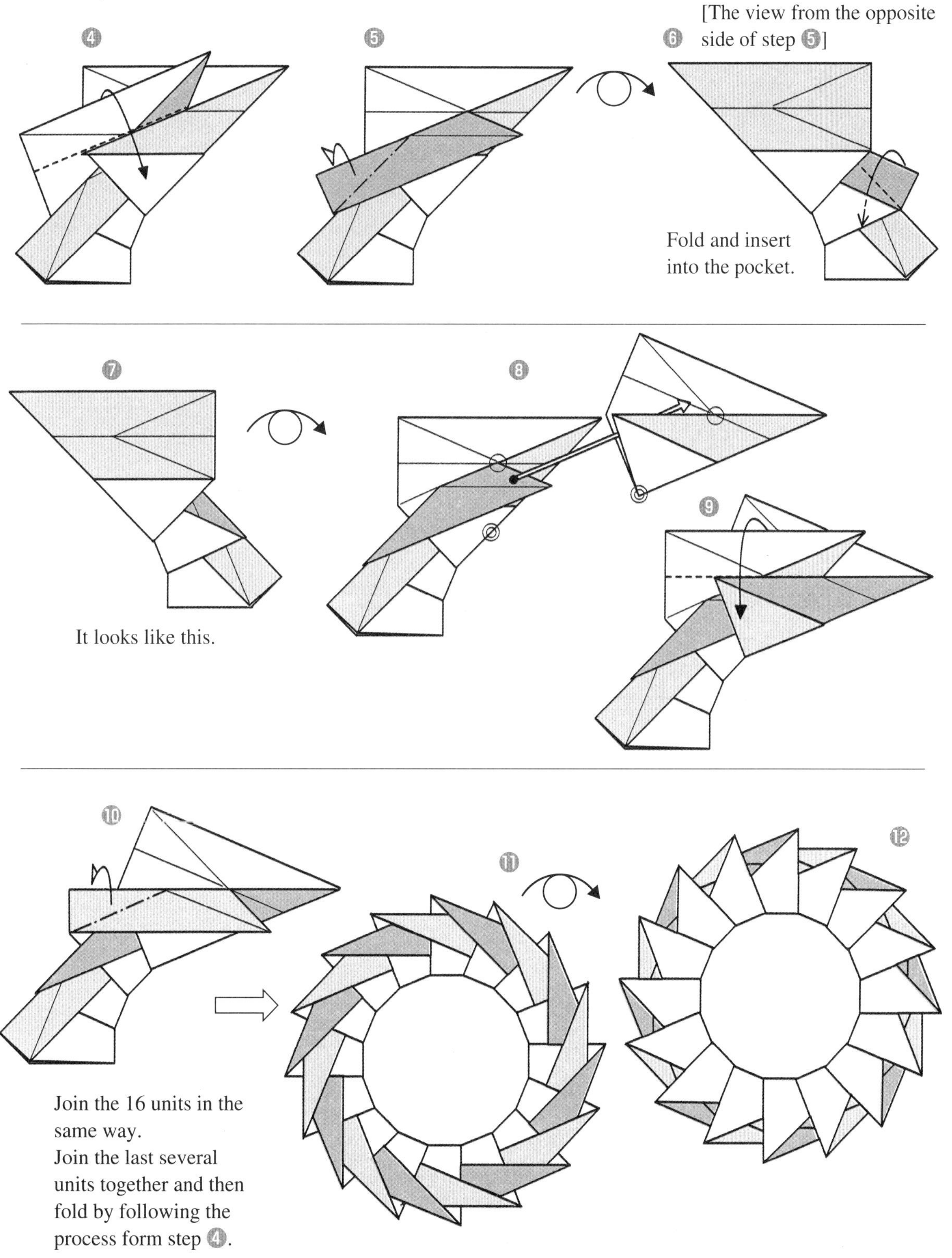
4
5
6
[The view from the opposite side of step 5]
Fold and insert into the pocket.
7
It looks like this.
8
9
10
11
12
Join the 16 units in the same way.
Join the last several units together and then fold by following the process form step 4.

# RING 9

Standard paper size:
7.5cm×7.5cm (3in×3in)

The patterns of the back and front sides are quite different.
The eight units are joined firmly.

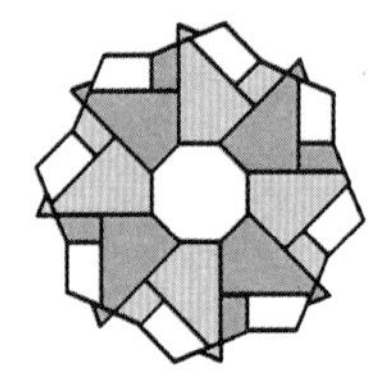

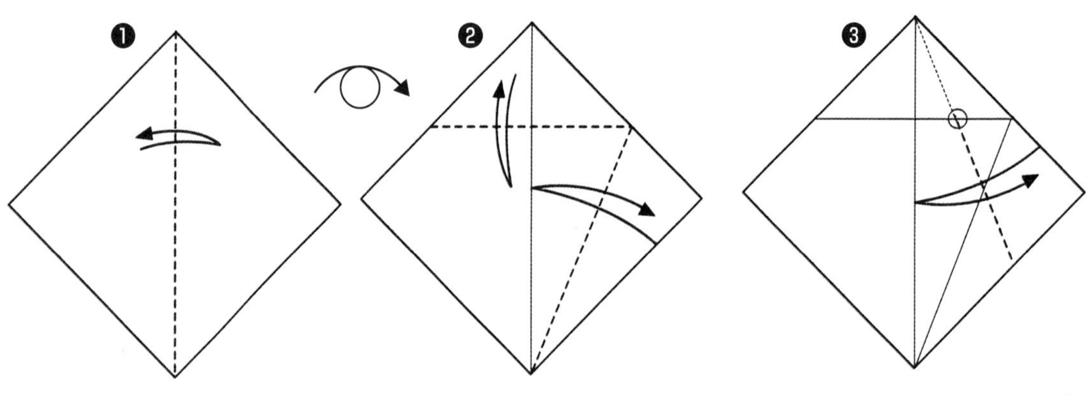


Make creases as shown.

Make a crease up to the circle ○.

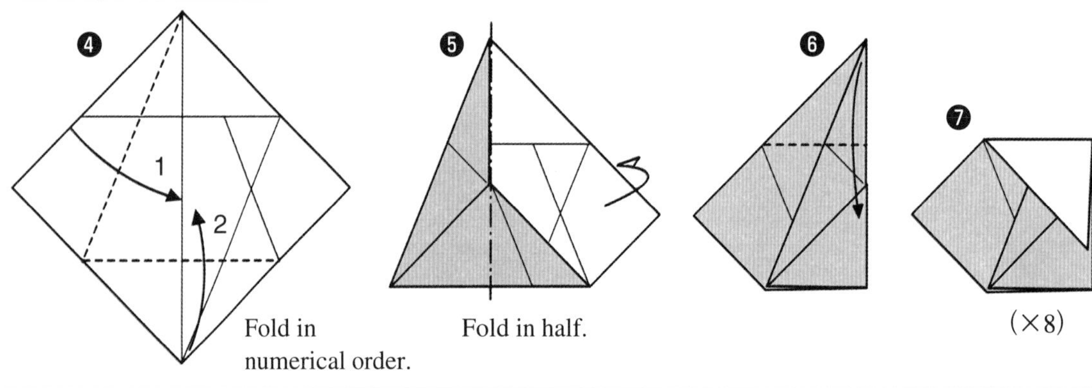


Fold in numerical order.

Fold in half.

(×8)

[Joining Method]

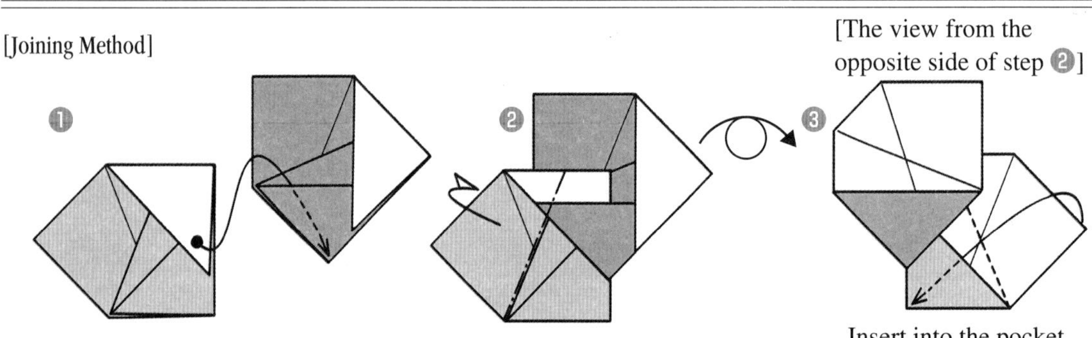


[The view from the opposite side of step ❷]

Insert into the pocket.

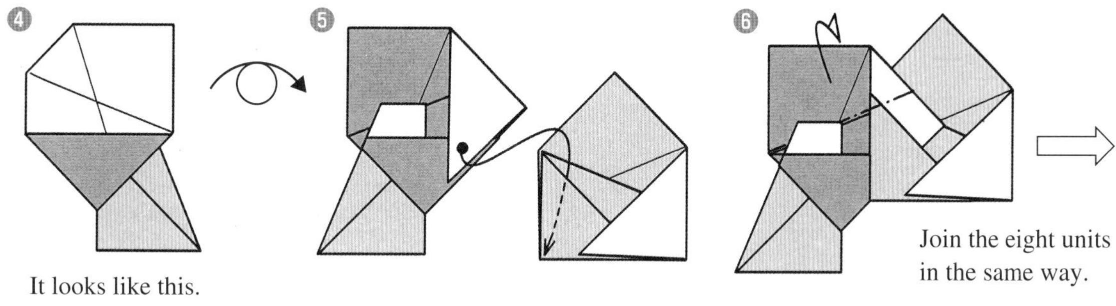


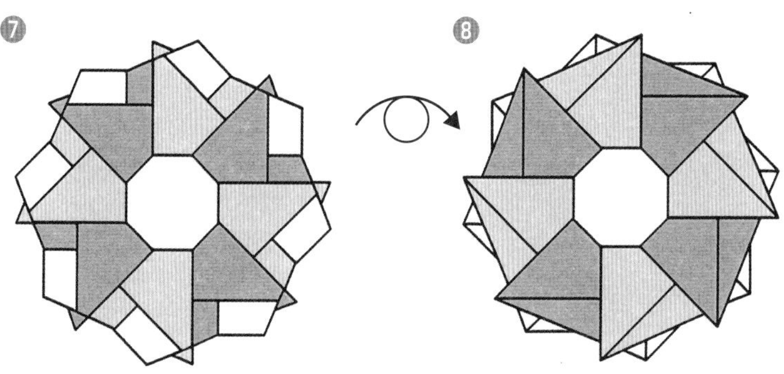

# RING 10

Standard paper size:
7.5cm×7.5cm (3 in×3 in)

This ring looks very complicated, but the methods of folding an joining are simple and easy. Use 16 units.

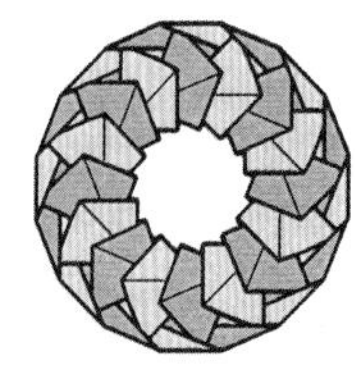

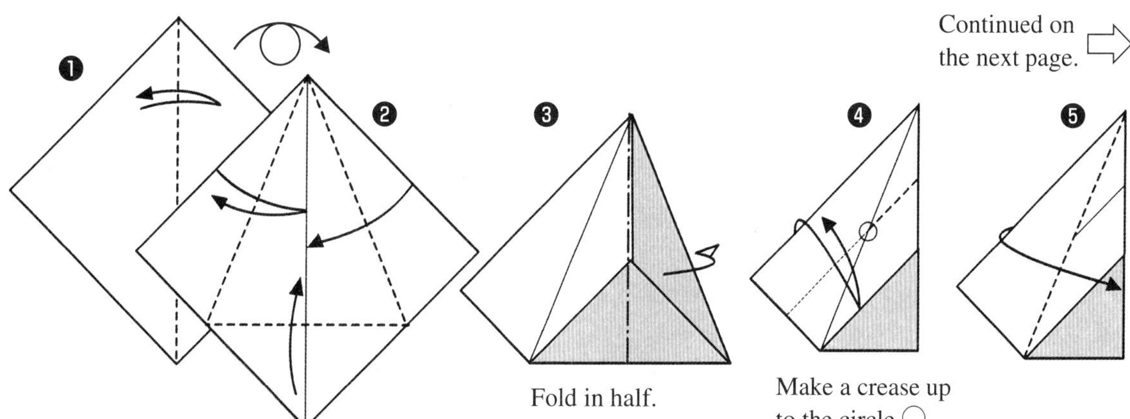


Continued on the next page.

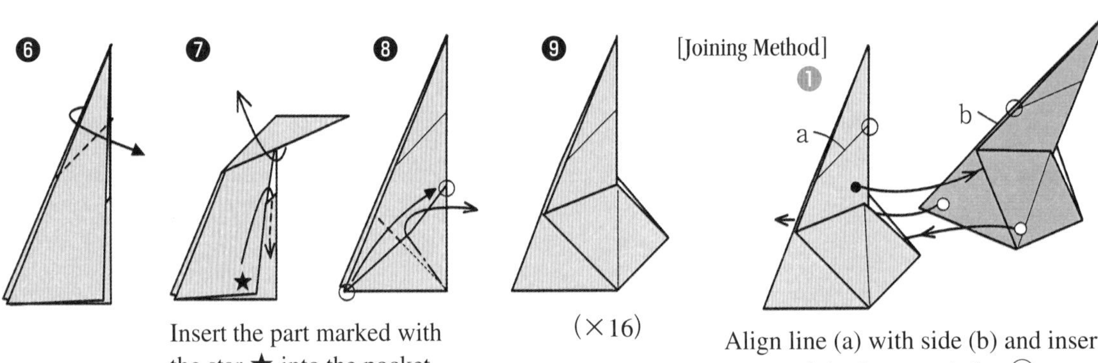


Insert the part marked with the star ★ into the pocket.

(×16)

Align line (a) with side (b) and insert so as to join the two circles ○.

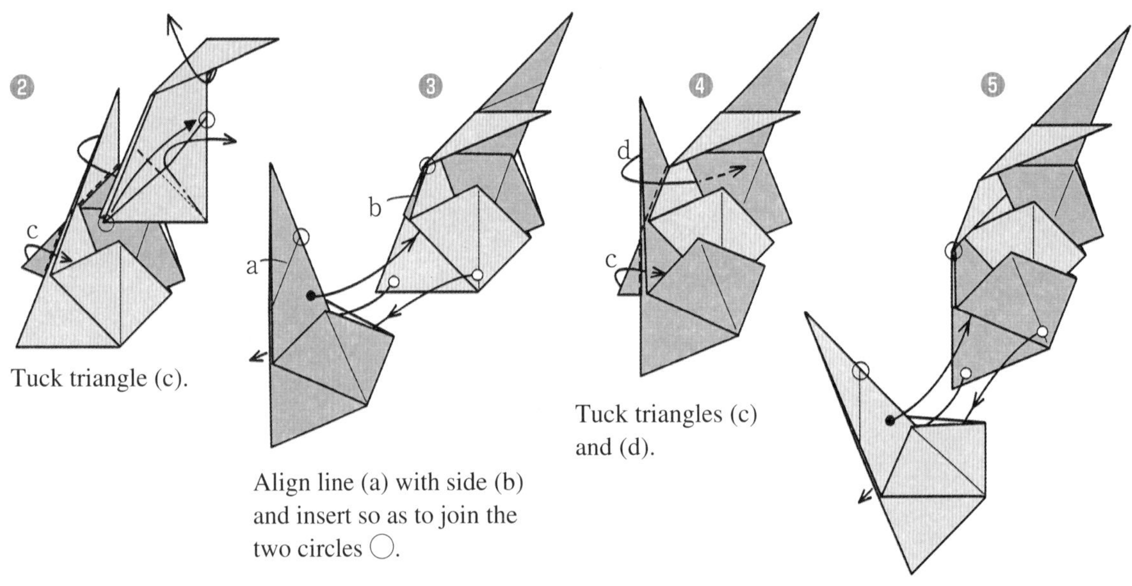


Tuck triangle (c).

Align line (a) with side (b) and insert so as to join the two circles ○.

Tuck triangles (c) and (d).

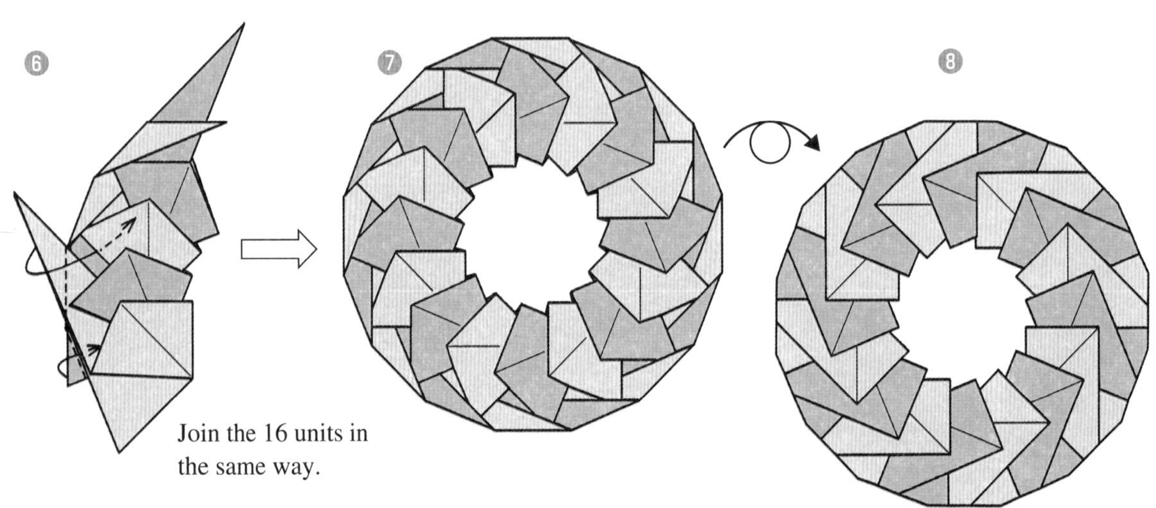


Join the 16 units in the same way.

# RING 11

Standard paper size:
7.5cm×7.5cm (3 in×3 in)

This ring is fixed firmly by joining method of step 5. Use 16 units.

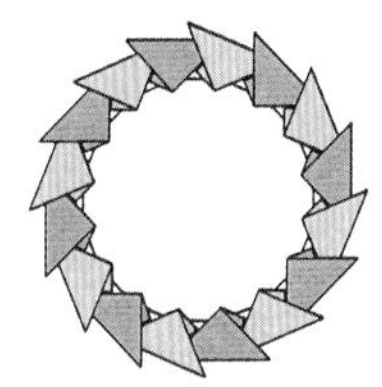

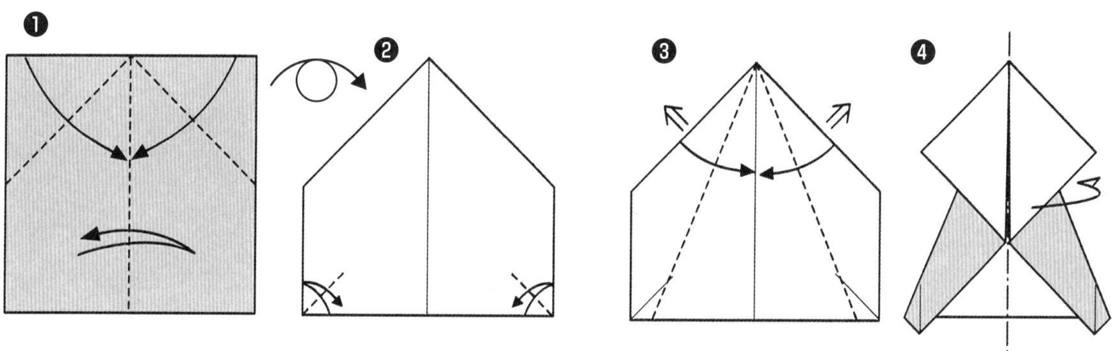


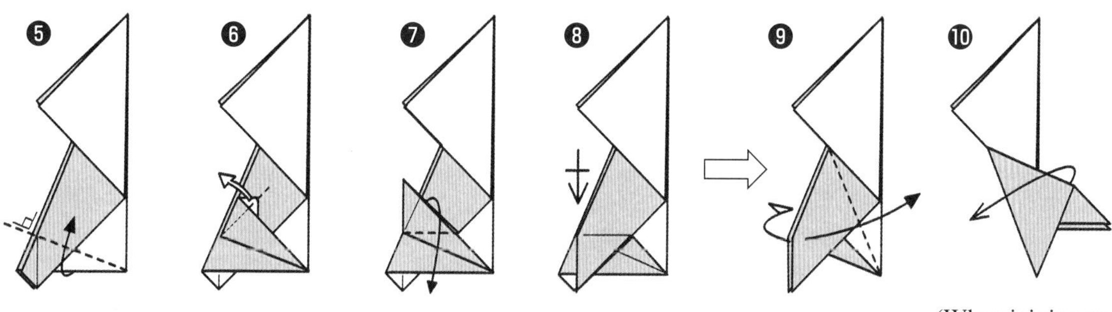


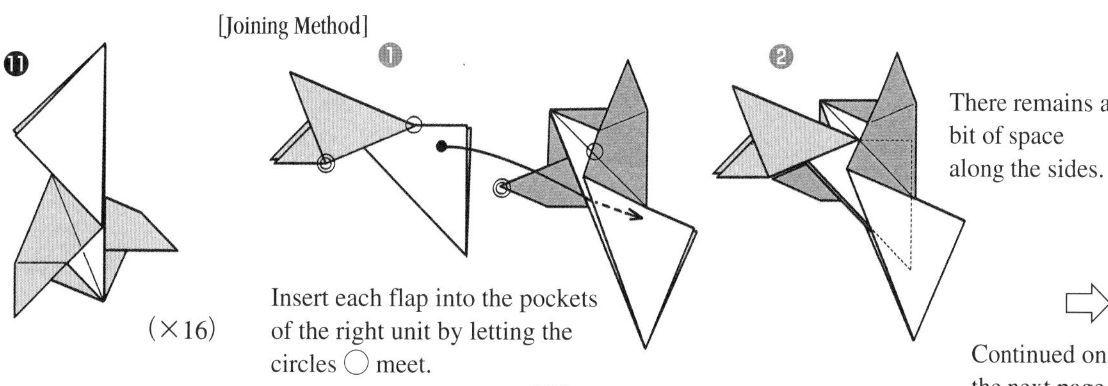


Continued on the next page.

3

4

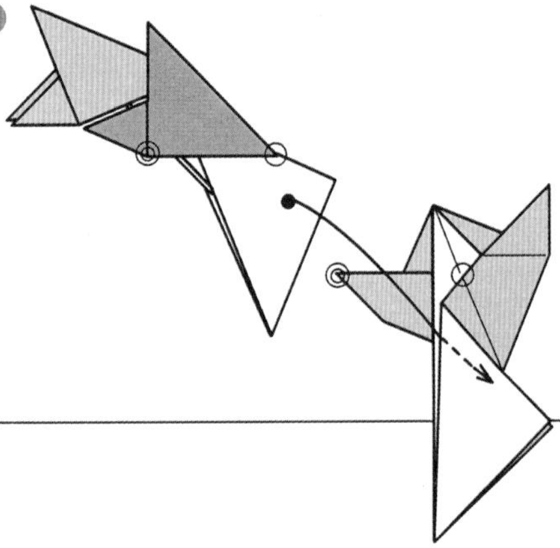

Join the 16 units
in the same way.

5

6

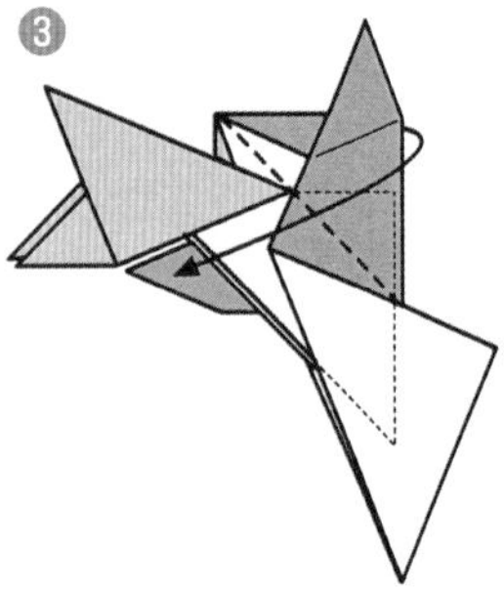

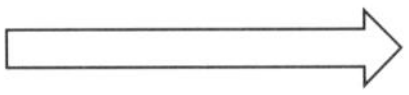

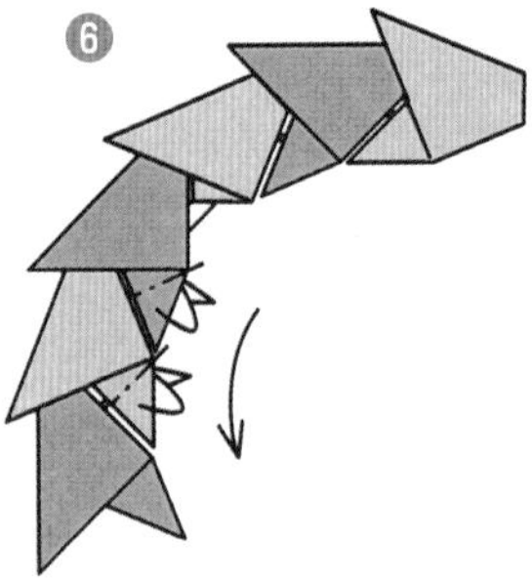

Tuck triangles one by one
as shown by the arrow.

7

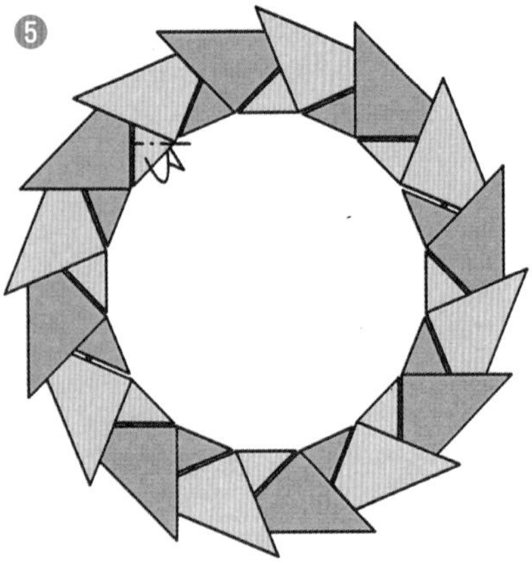

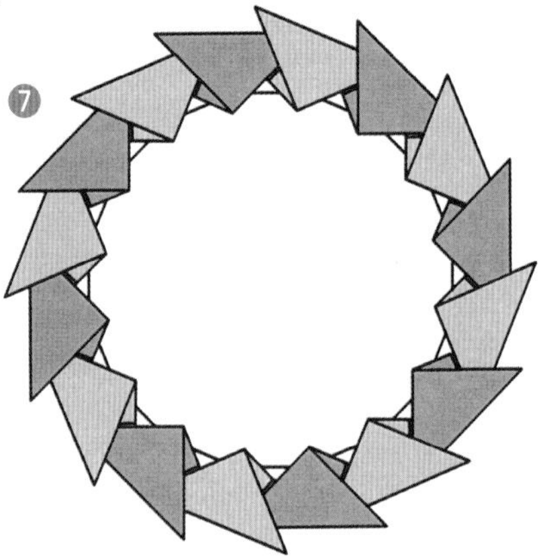

# RING 12

Standard paper size:
7.5cm × 7.5cm (3 in × 3 in)

When folding, steps ❿-⓬ are important points.
When joining, the tucking in step ❷.
makes this ring firm.

1

2

3

4

5

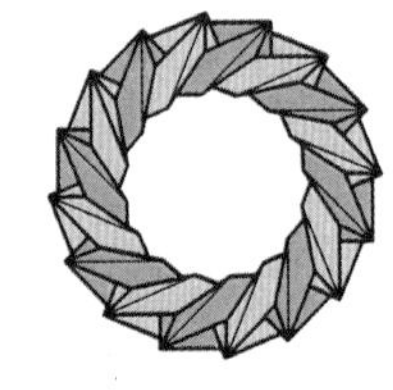

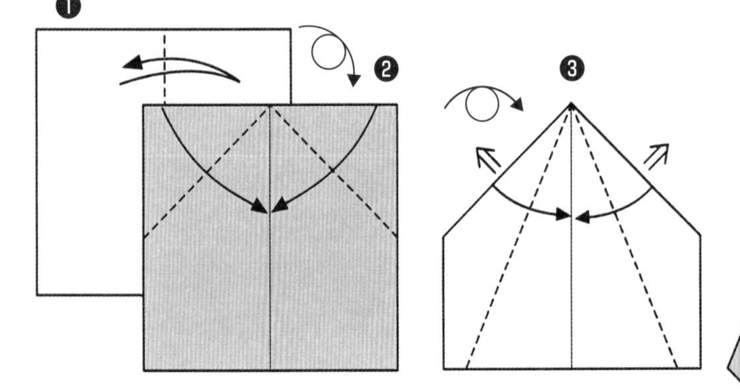

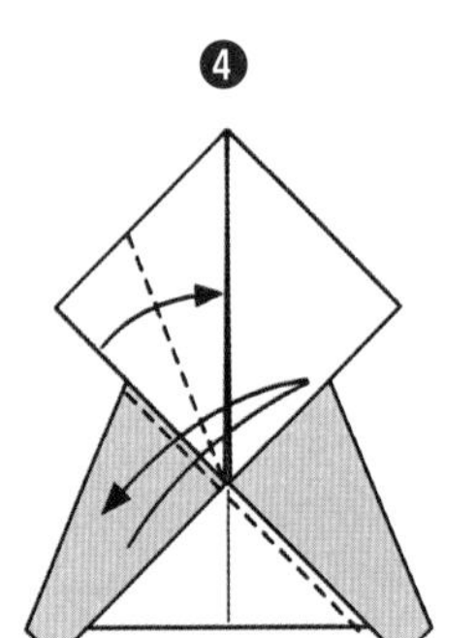

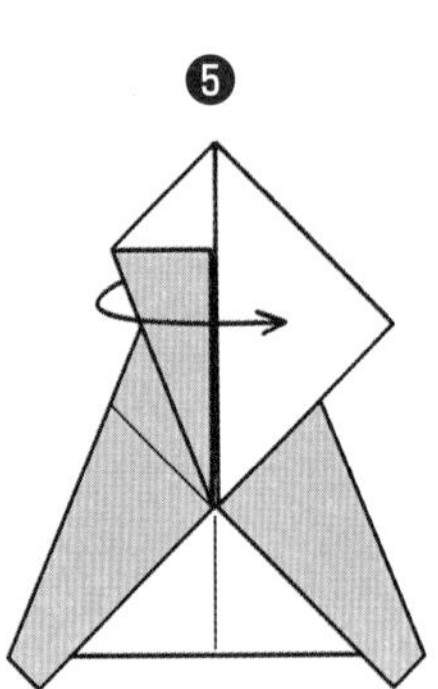

6

7

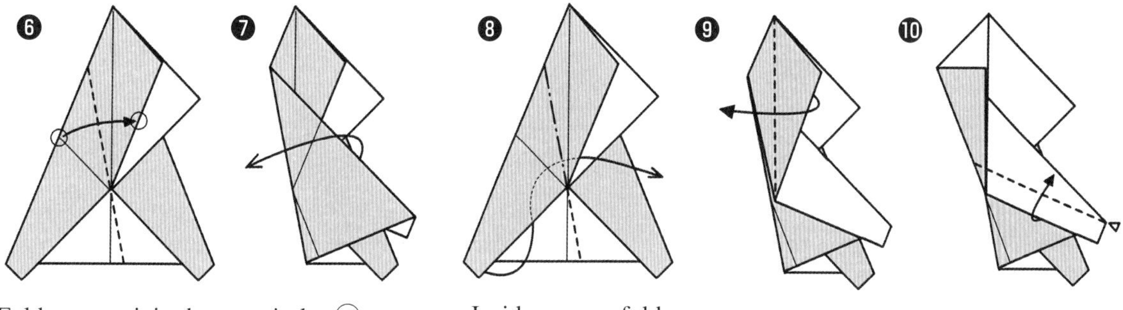

Fold so as to join the two circles ◯.

8

Inside reverse fold.

9

10

11

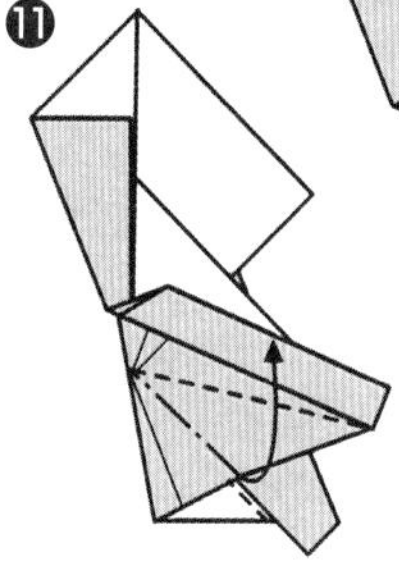

12

Put the part marked with the star ★ under the rectangle part.

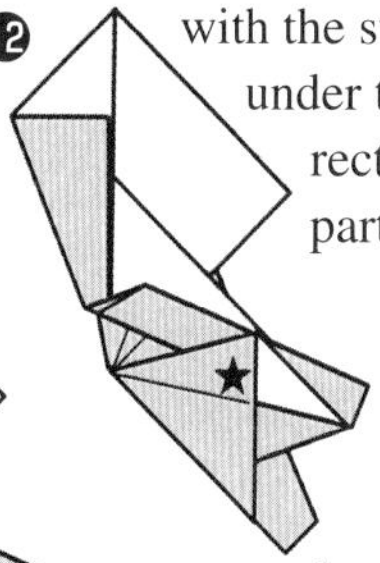

13

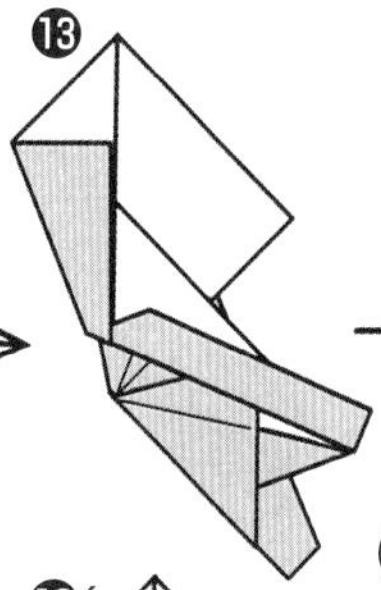

(×1)

13´

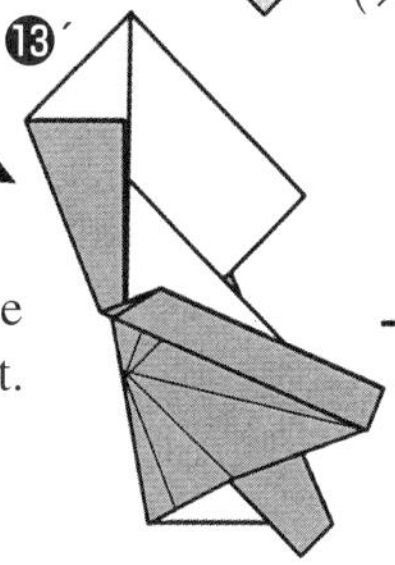

Unfold the under part.

(×15)

[Joining Method]

1

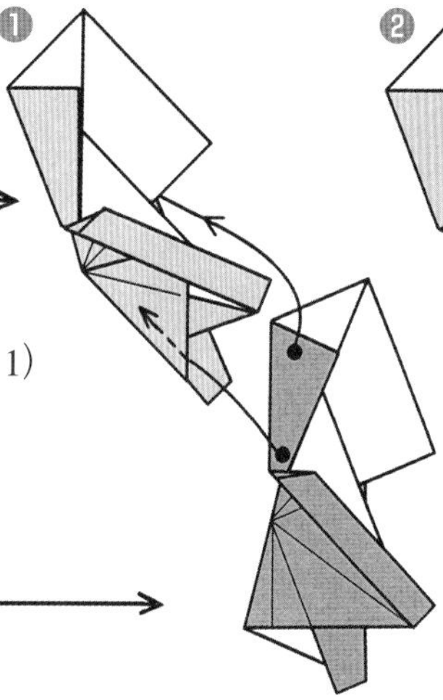

2

Tuck into the pocket.

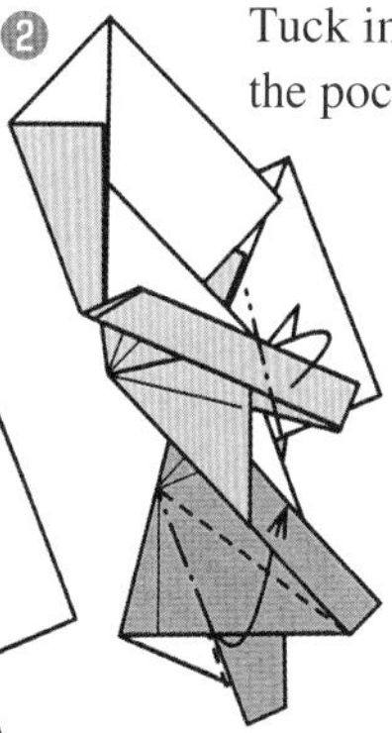

Fold in the same was as steps 11- 13.

3

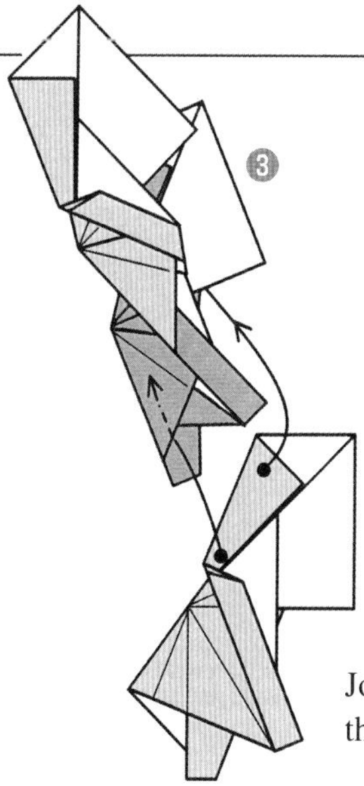

Join the 16 units in the same way.

4

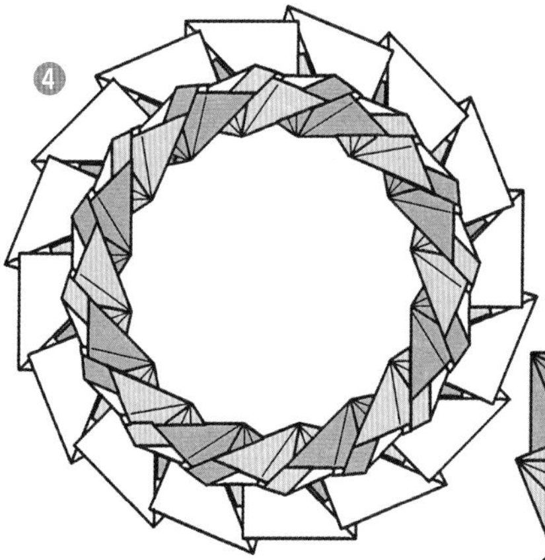

5

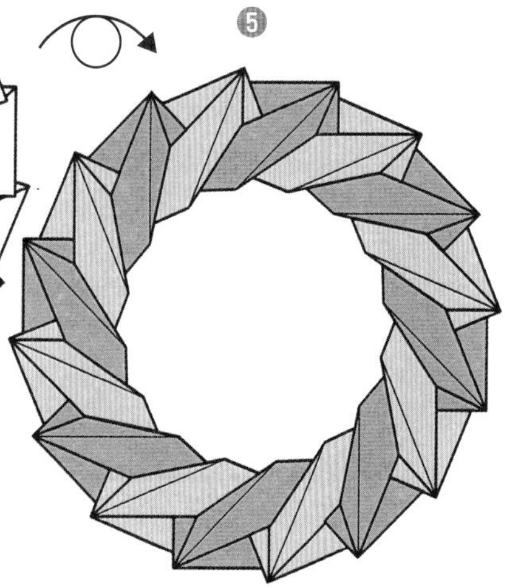

# RING 13

Standard paper size:
7.5cm×7.5cm (3 in×3 in)

You may have two types of rings, (A) with horns and (B) without horns.

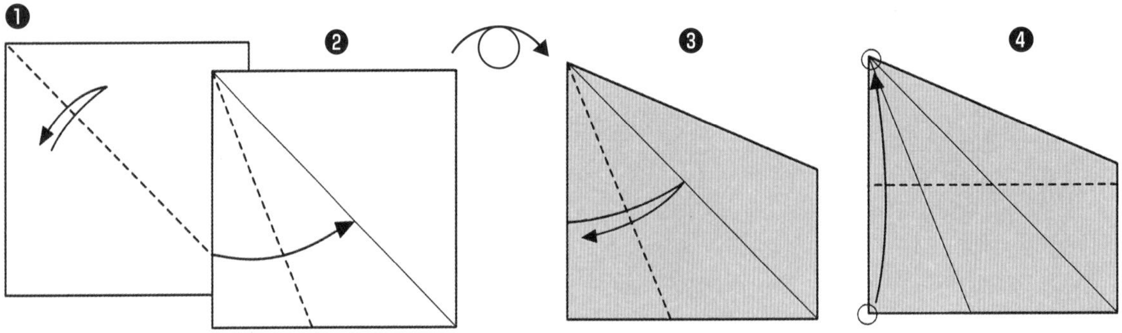

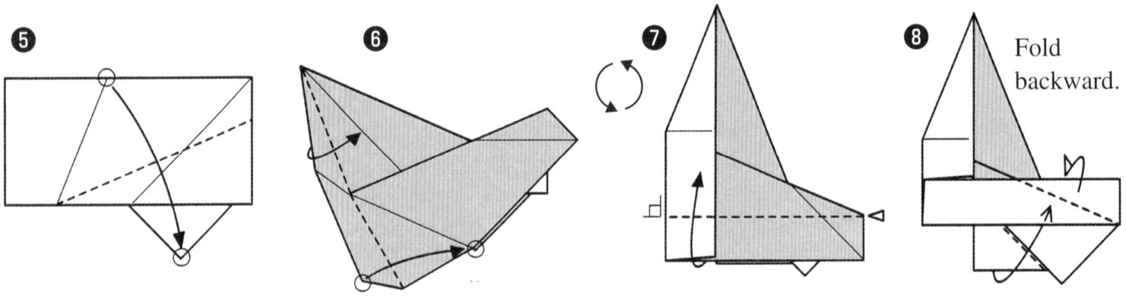

❶ ❷ ❸ ❹

❺ ❻ ❼ ❽

Fold backward.

Fold so as to join the two circles ○.

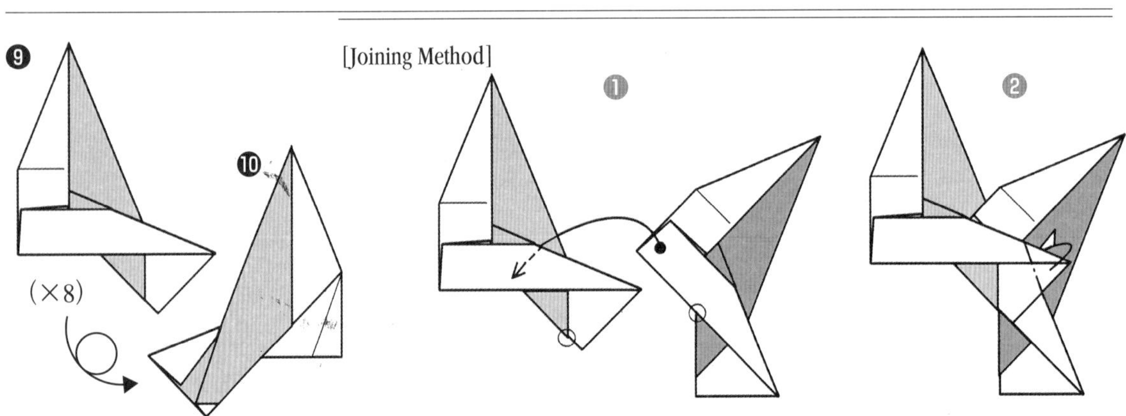


[The view from the opposite side.]

Insert so as to join the two circles ○.

Tuck the tip.

3

Join the eight units in the same way.

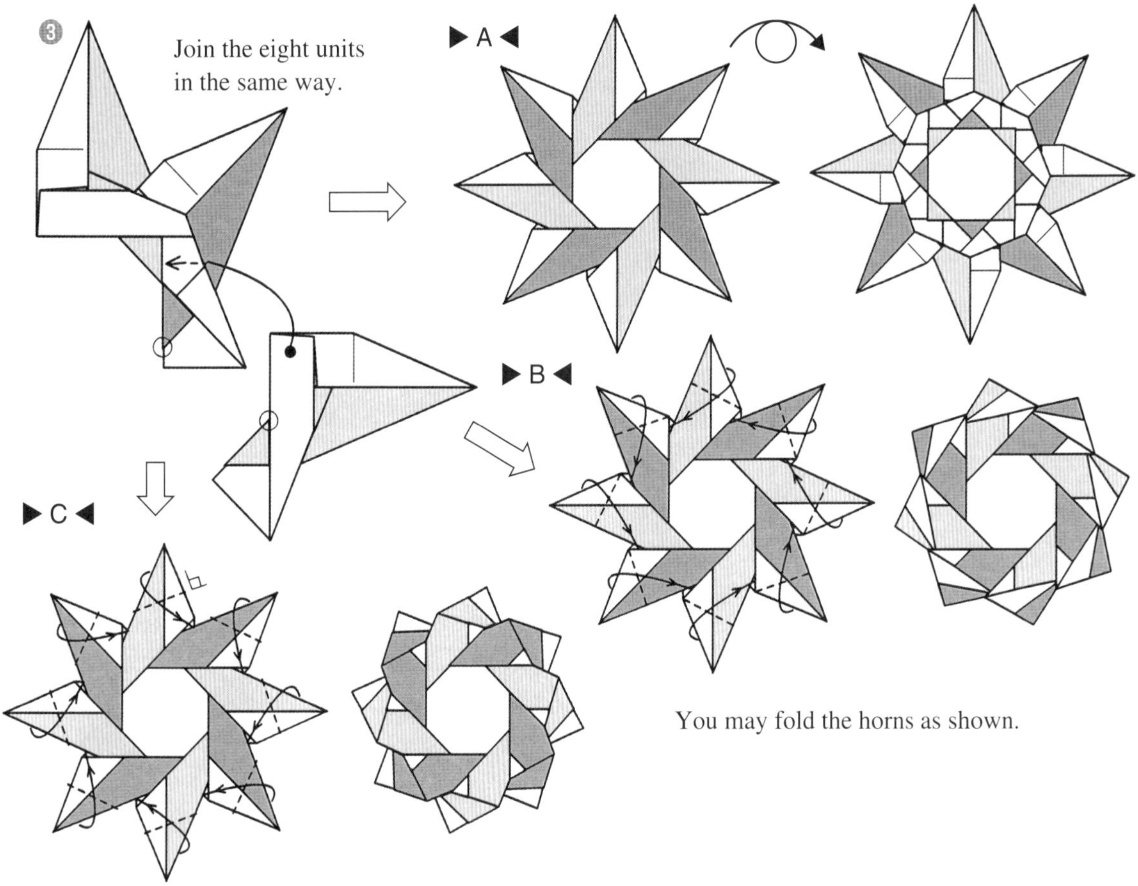

▶A◀

▶B◀

▶C◀

You may fold the horns as shown.

# RING 14

Paper size:
5cm×5cm (2 in×2 in) or smaller than this.

You may use smaller paper to make the hole large.
Use 16 units.

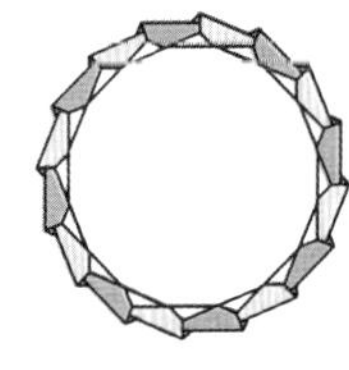

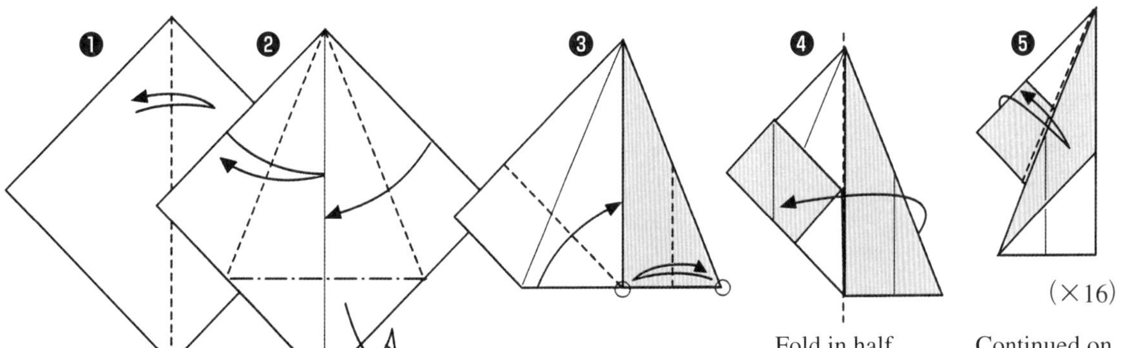


Continued on the next page.

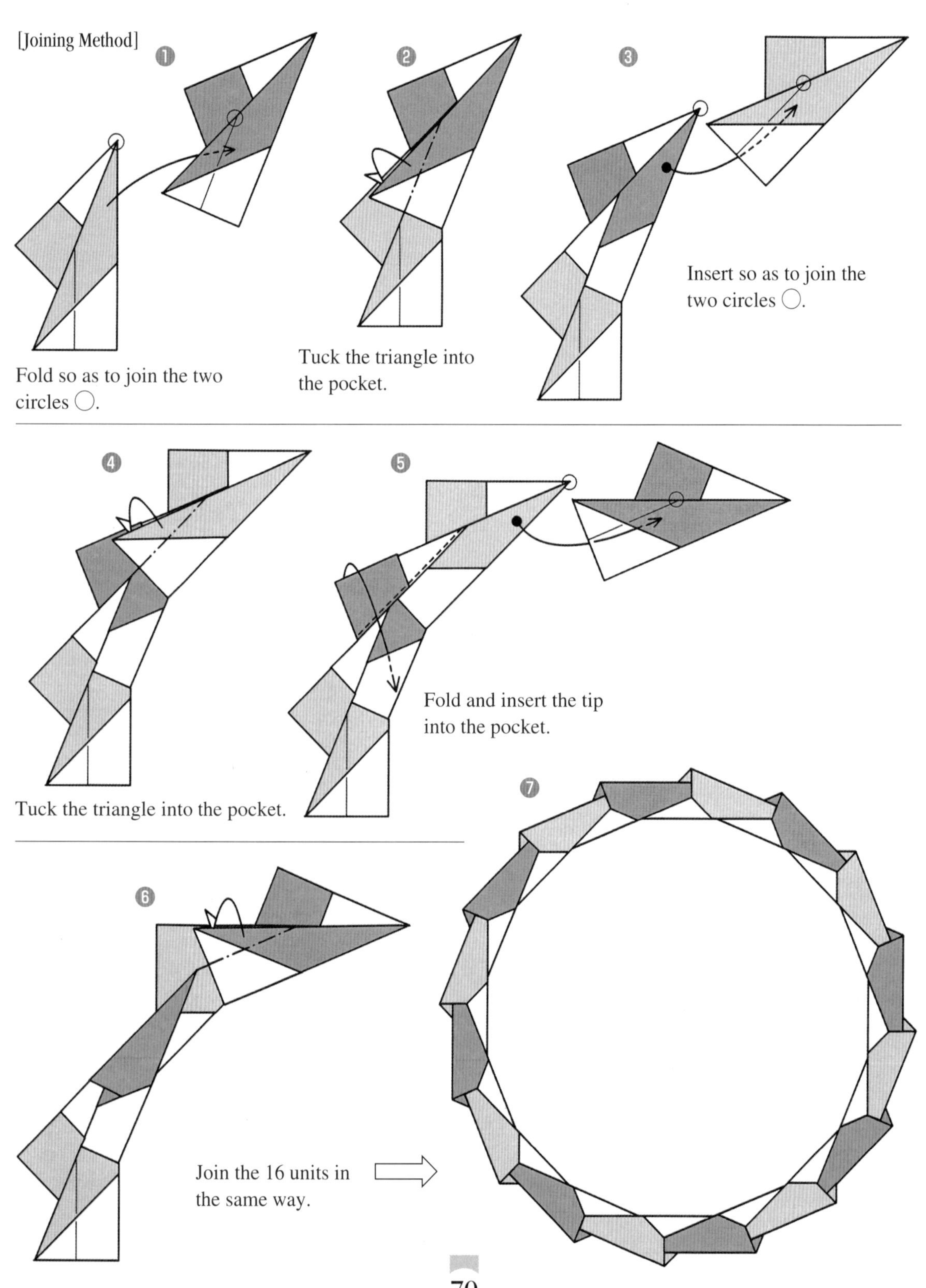
[Joining Method]
1
Fold so as to join the two circles ◯.
2
Tuck the triangle into the pocket.
3
Insert so as to join the two circles ◯.
4
Tuck the triangle into the pocket.
5
Fold and insert the tip into the pocket.
6
Join the 16 units in the same way.
7

# RING 15

**Standard paper size:**
**7.5cm×7.5cm (3 in×3 in)**

The purpose to fold the corner in step ❹ is to avoid getting stuck when joining.
The folding position does not need to be exact.
You can also have a plain ring.

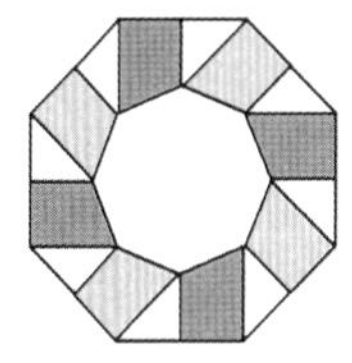

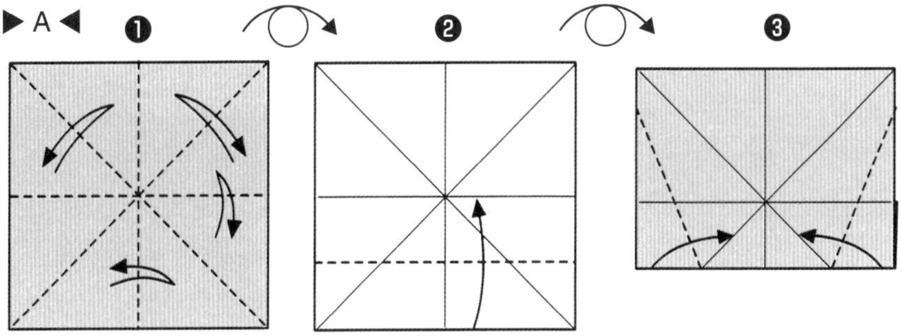

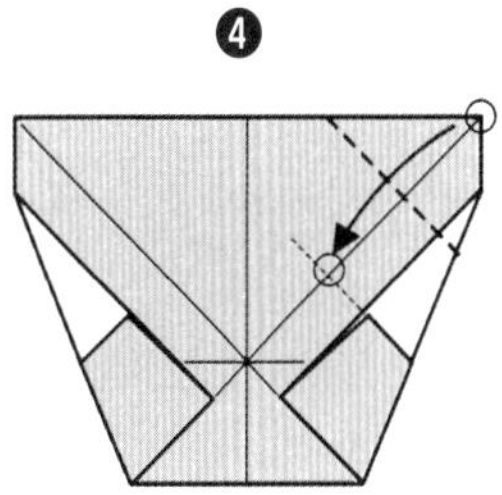

▶A◀ ❶ ❷ ❸ ❹

The folding position does not need to be exact.

❺ ❻ ❼ ❽

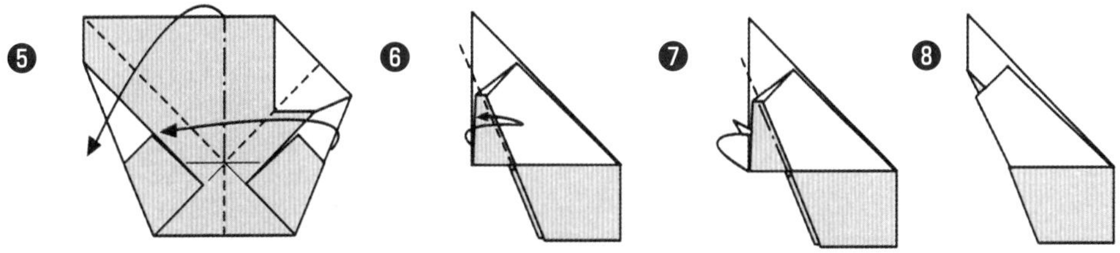

Fold together according to the creases.

Inside reverse fold.

(×8)

[Joining Method]

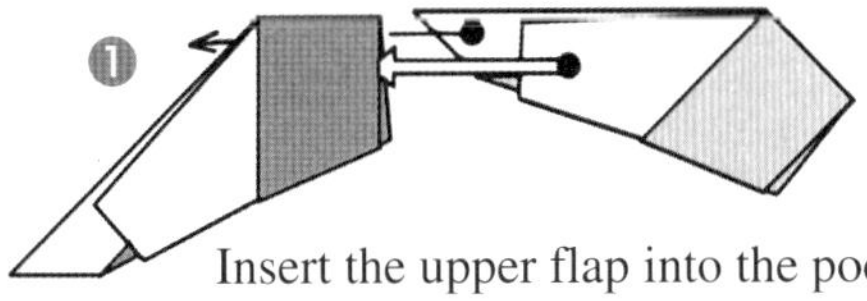

❶ Insert the upper flap into the pocket and put the outside flap behind.

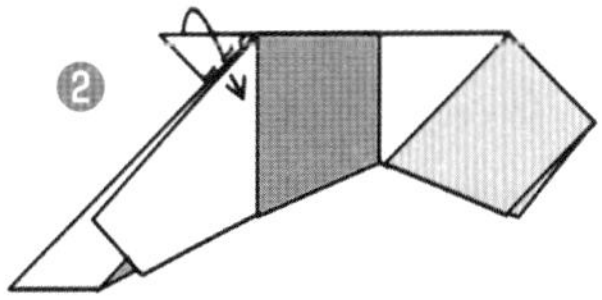

❷ Fix by tucking.

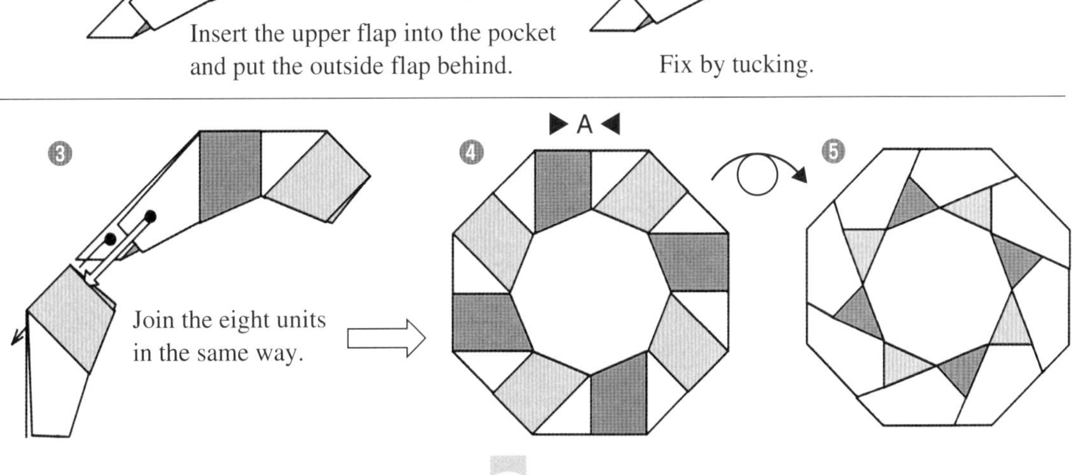

▶ B: Plain ◀

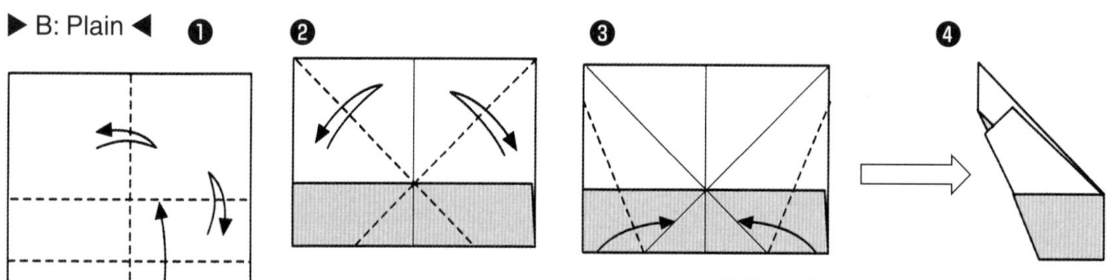


Follow the methods of folding and joining in the same way as from step ❹.

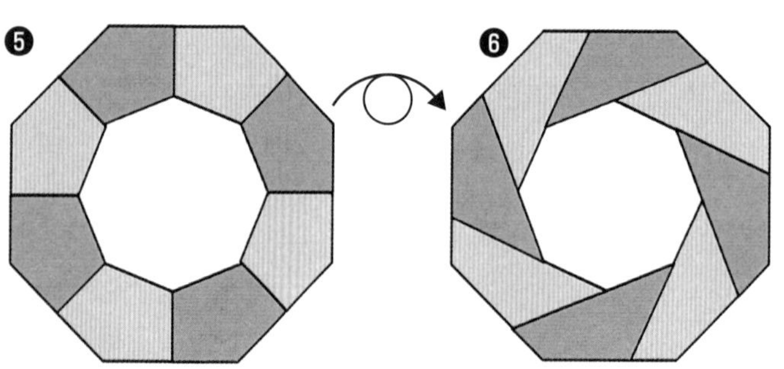


# RING 16

Standard paper size:
7.5cm×7.5cm (3 in×3 in)

Use 12 units. The angles have play but you can fix the units nicely.

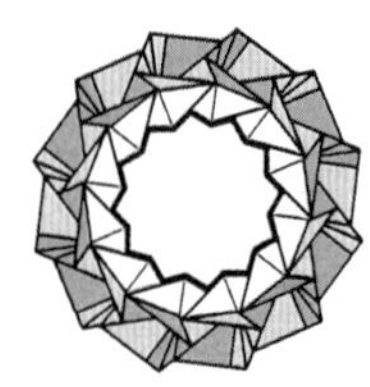

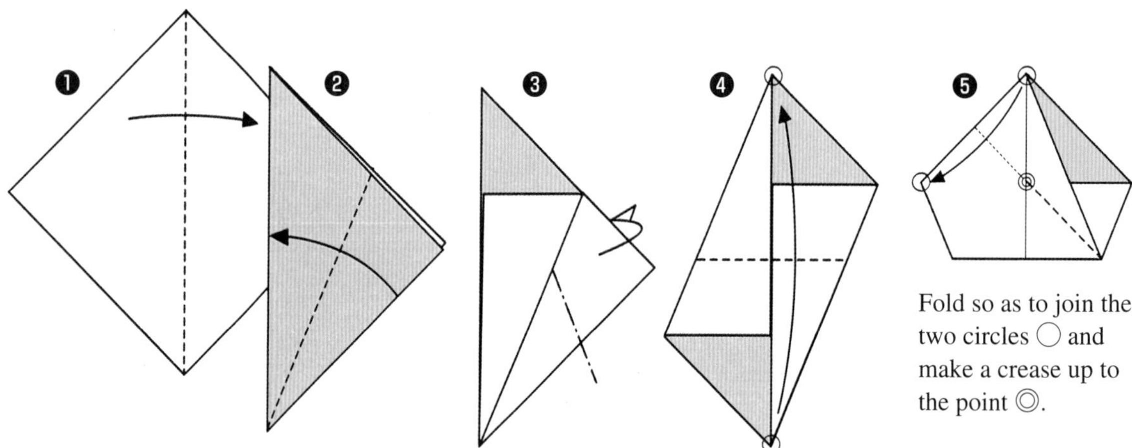


Fold so as to join the two circles ○ and make a crease up to the point ◎.

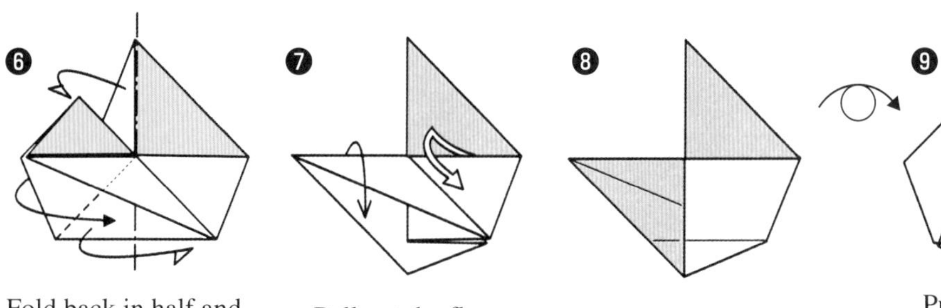

6 Fold back in half and flatten the left triangle.

7 Pull out the flap.

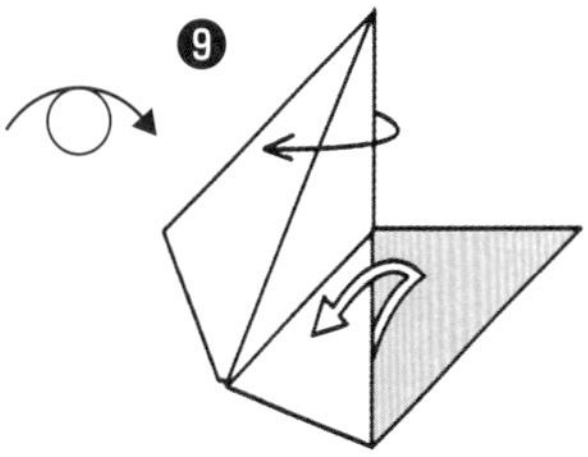

8

9 Pull out the flap.

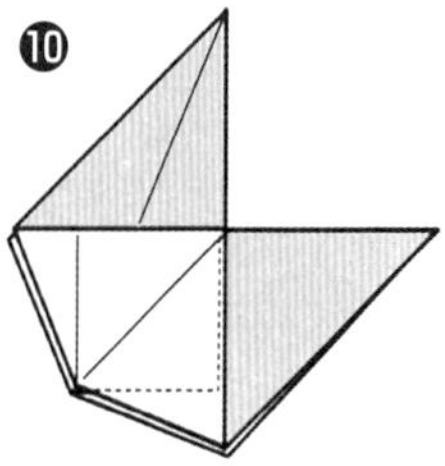

10 (×12)

[Joining Method]

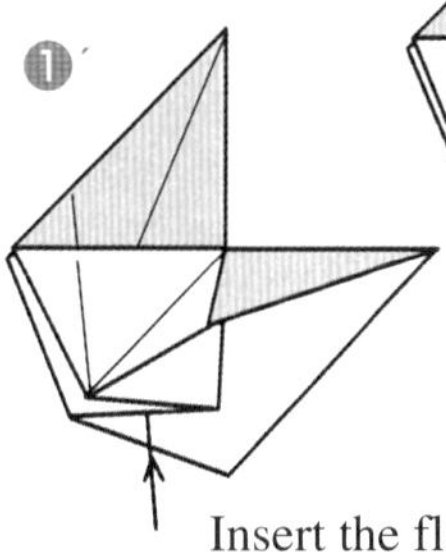

1′ Insert the flap (a) into the bottom.

1 Insert by joining the two circles ○.

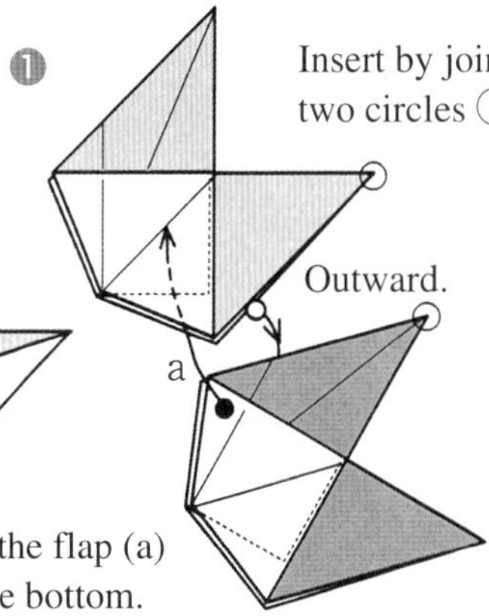

Outward.

a

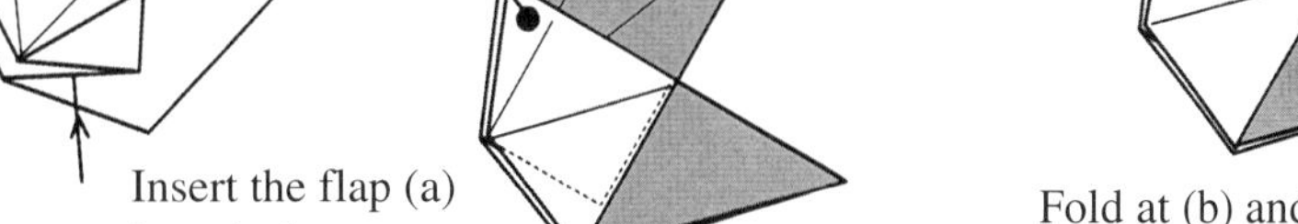

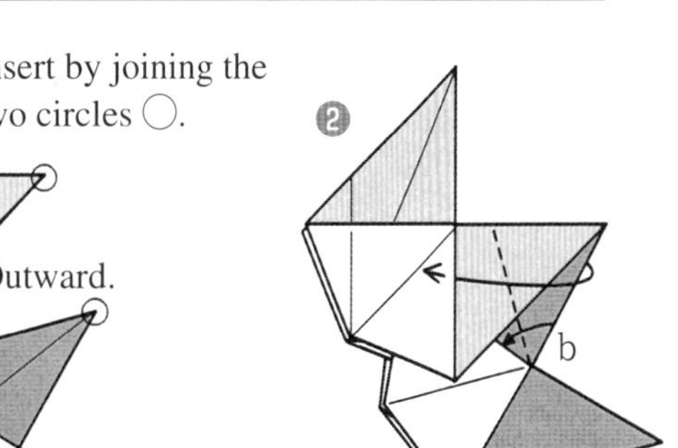


2 Fold at (b) and insert into the pocket.

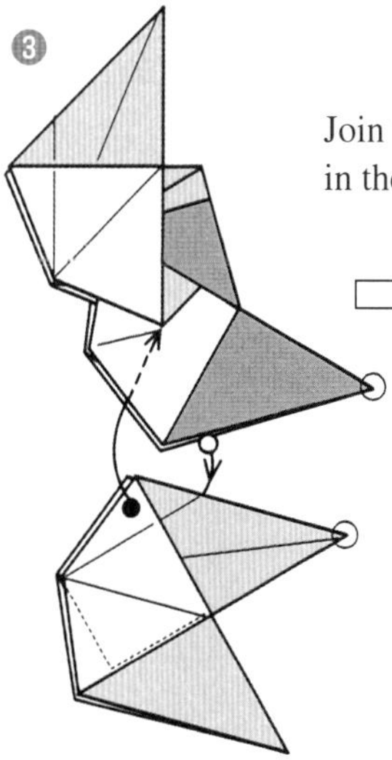

3

▶A◀

Join the 12 units in the same way.

4

5

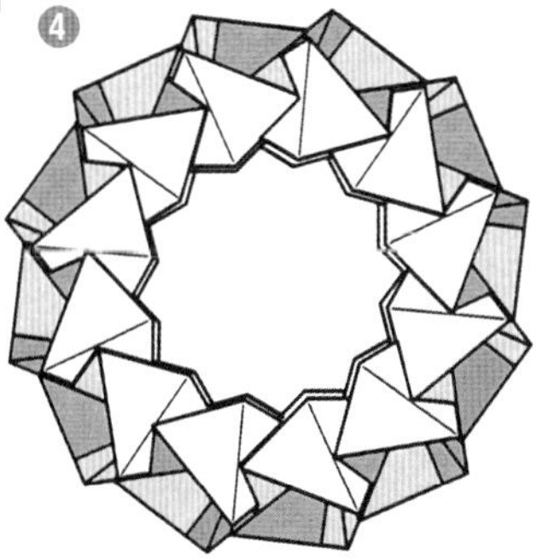

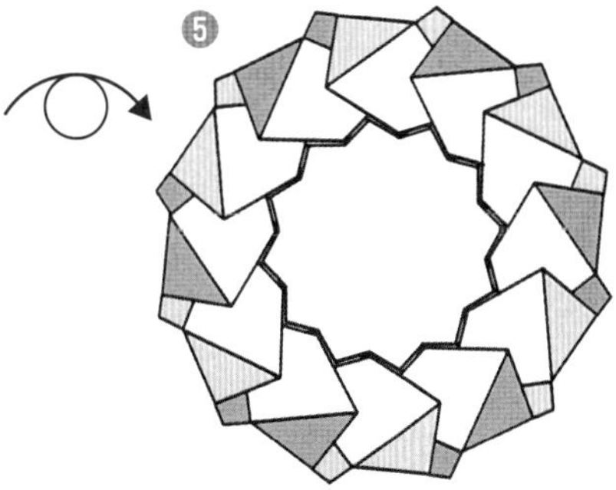

▶B◀

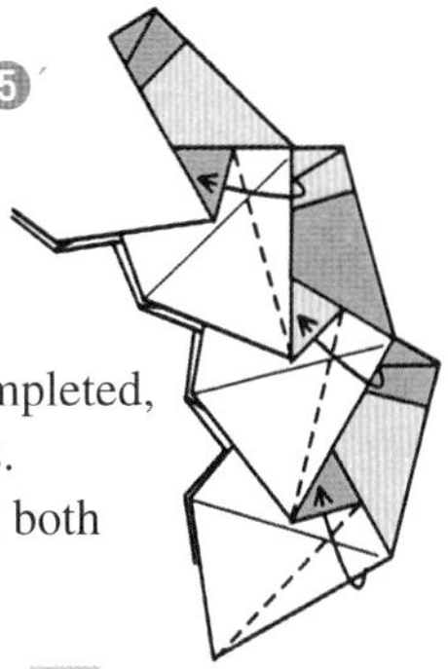

5′ After A is completed, fold the edges. You may fold both sides.

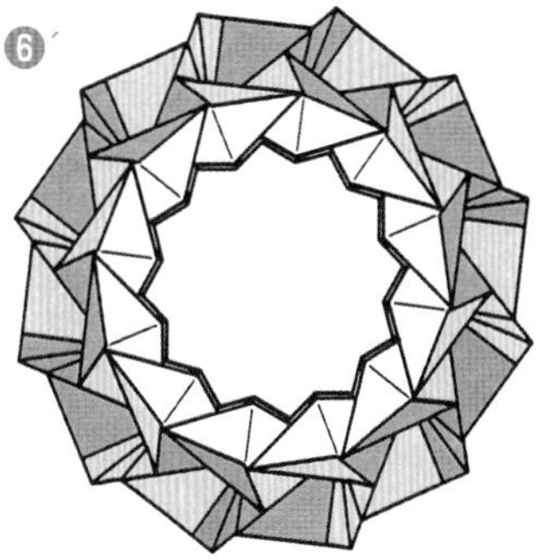

6′

# RING 17

Standard paper size:
7.5cm×7.5cm (3 in×3 in)

It is possible to make a ring of different color or mixed color.

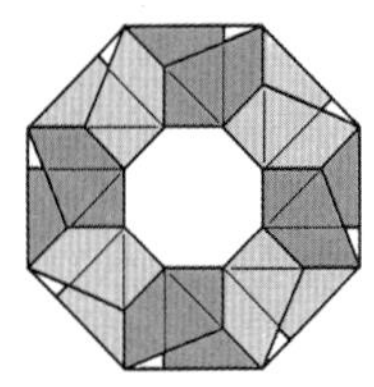

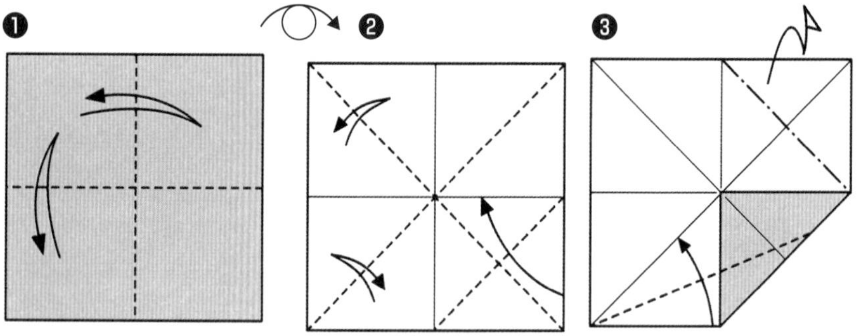

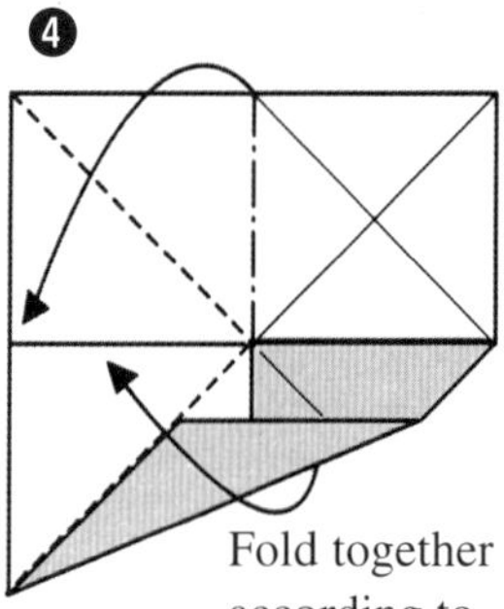

❶ ❷ ❸ ❹

Fold together according to the creases.

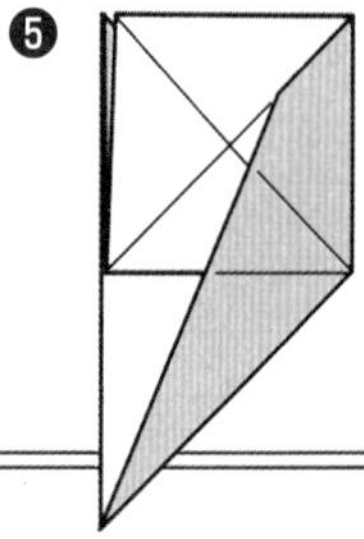

❺

(×8)

[Joining Method]

➊

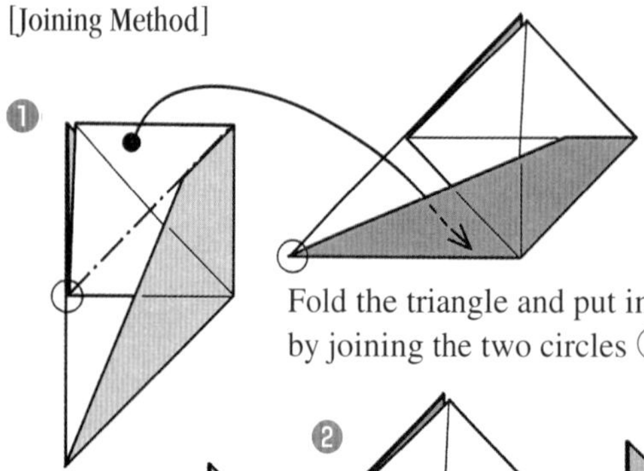

Fold the triangle and put into the pocket by joining the two circles ○.

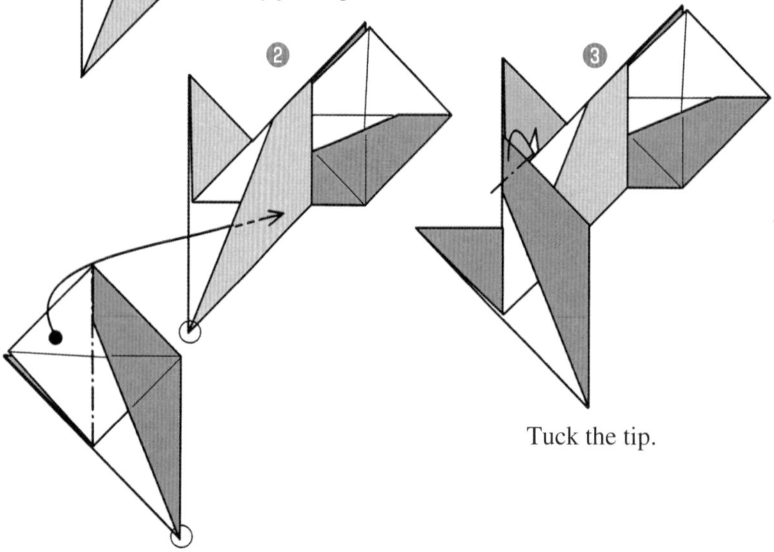

➋ ➌ ➍

Tuck the tip.

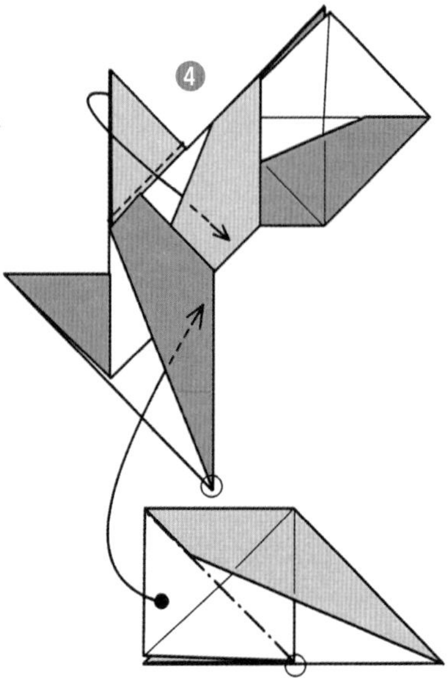

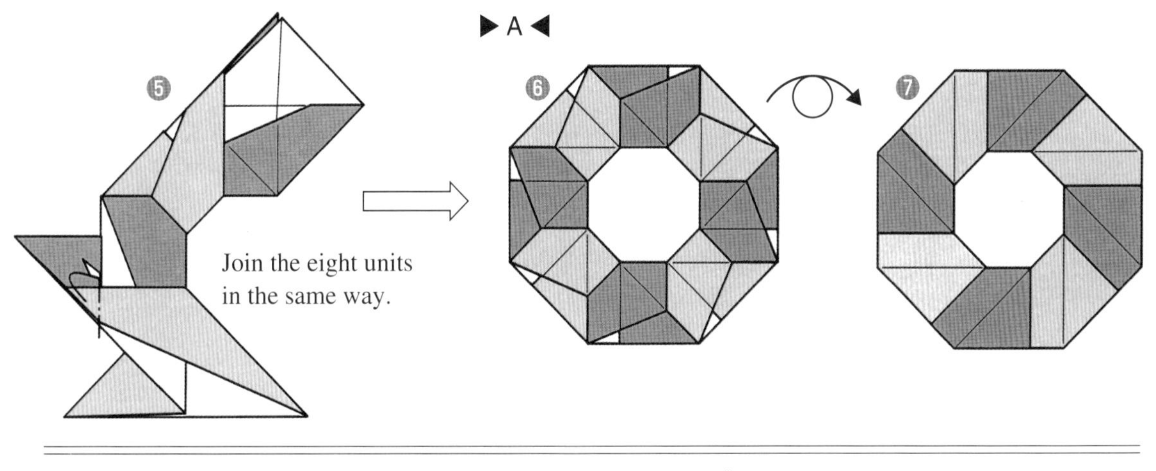


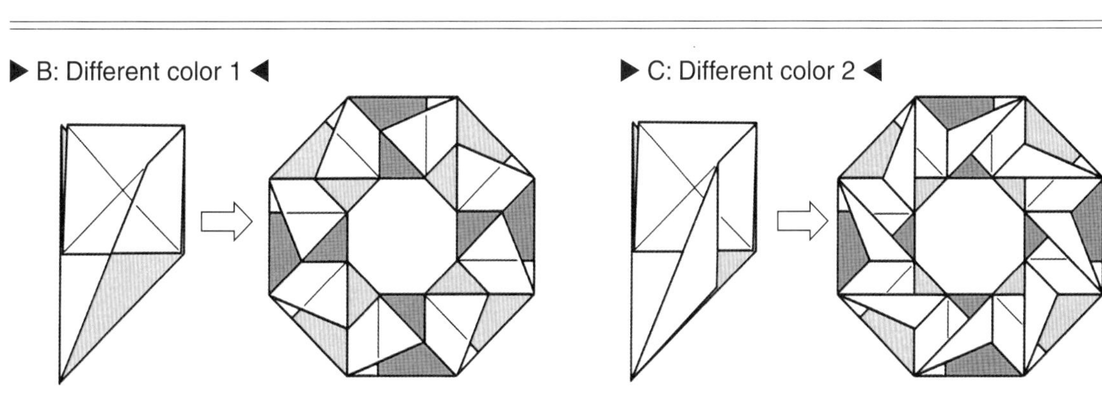


# RING 18

Standard paper size:
7.5cm×7.5cm (3in×3in)

This is the brother of Ring 17. Use 16 units.
You can make a ring of different color.

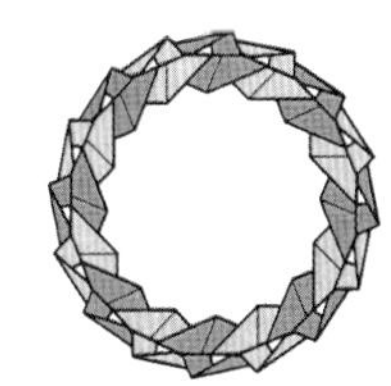

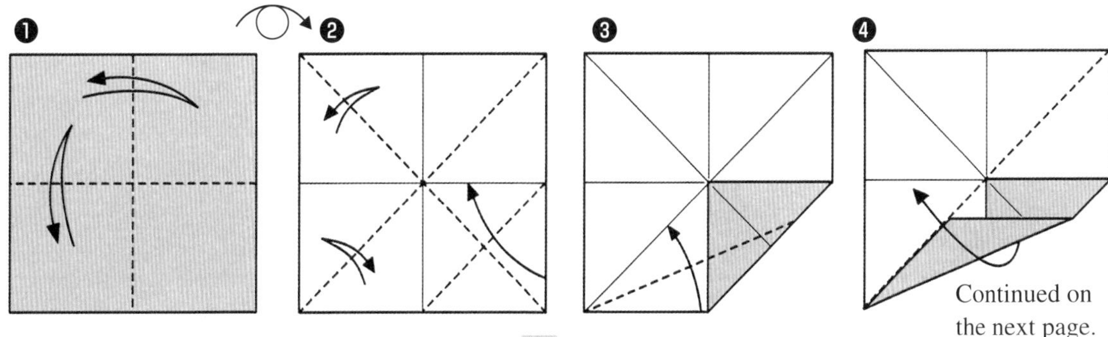

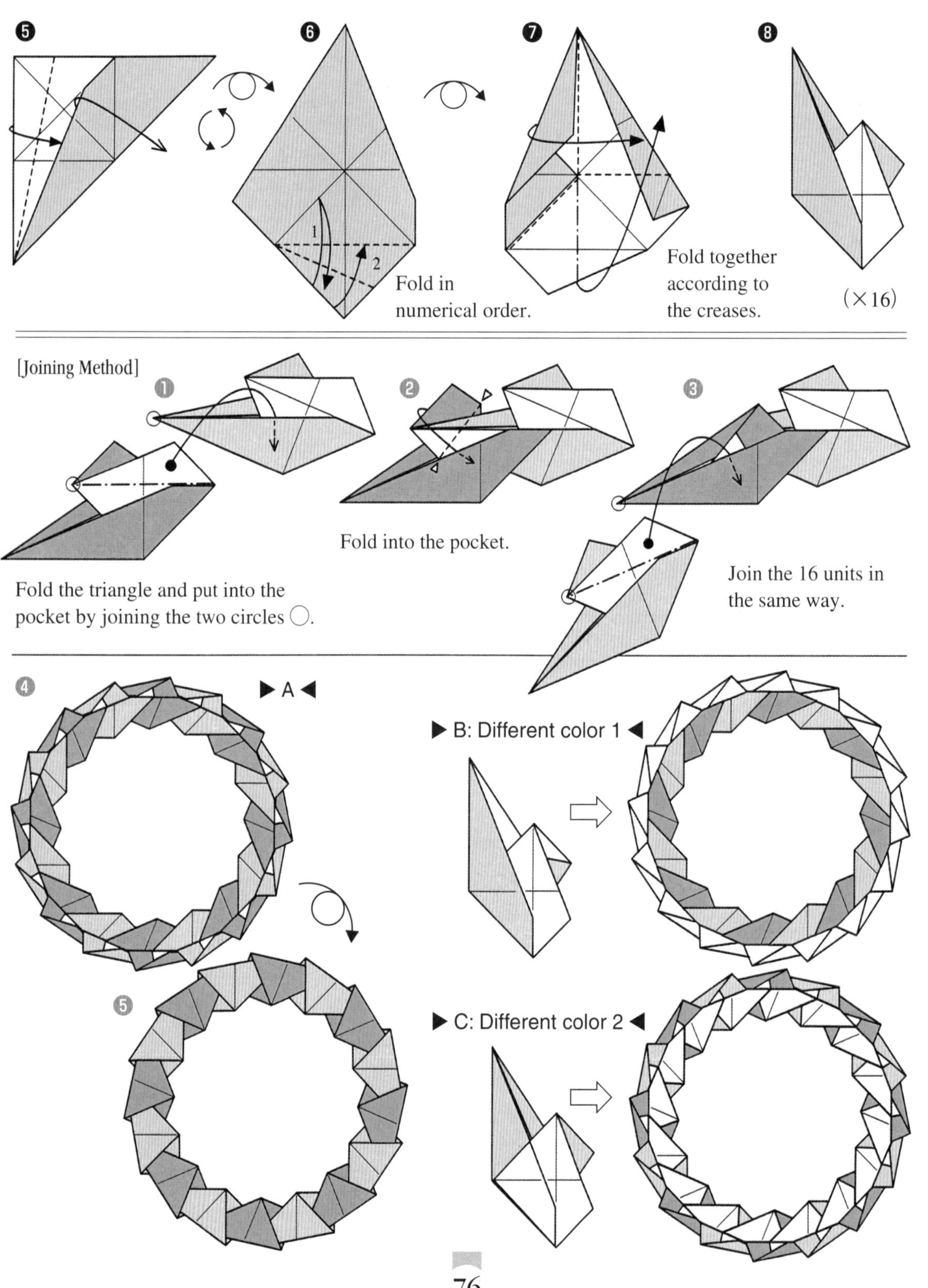
5
6
1
2
Fold in numerical order.
7
Fold together according to the creases.
8
(×16)
[Joining Method]
1
Fold the triangle and put into the pocket by joining the two circles ○.
2
Fold into the pocket.
3
Join the 16 units in the same way.
4
▶ A ◀
5
▶ B: Different color 1 ◀
▶ C: Different color 2 ◀

# RING 19

Standard paper size:
7.5cm×7.5cm (3 in×3 in)

There are two joining methods, A and B, and it is possible to employ different methods for back and front.

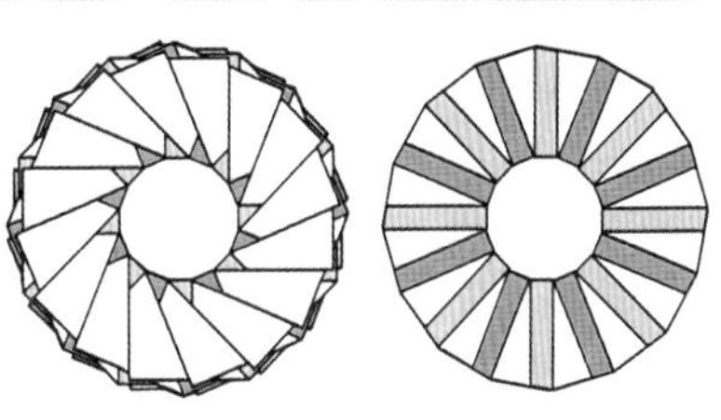

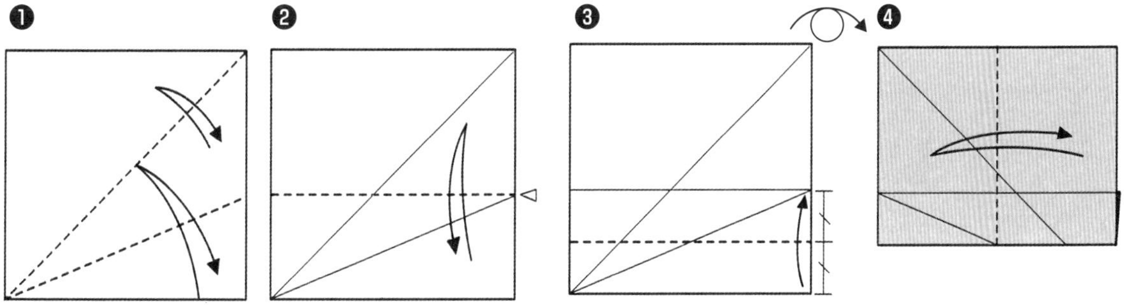

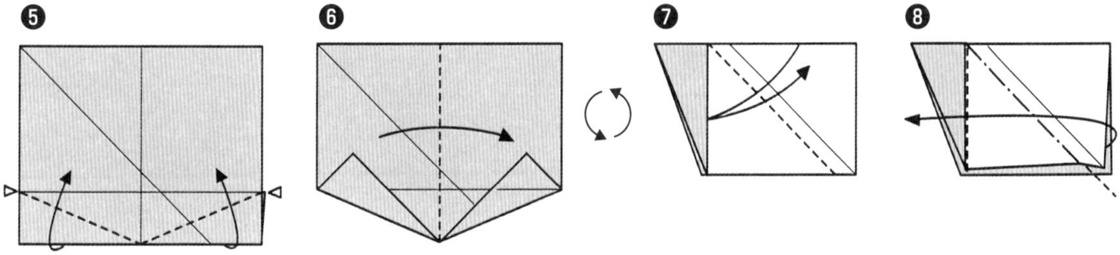

❶ ❷ ❸ ❹

❺ ❻ ❼ ❽

Fold in half.

▶ A ◀

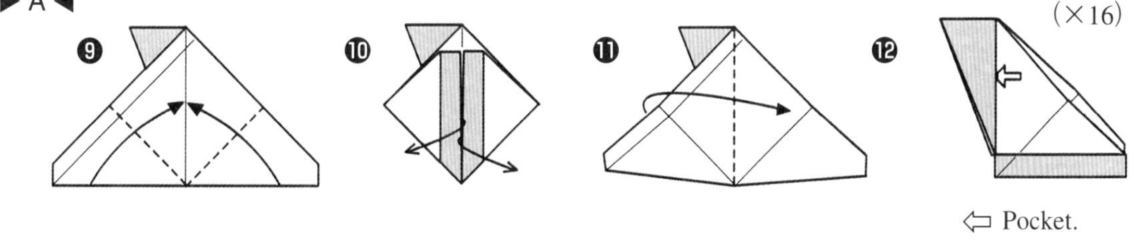


▶ B ◀

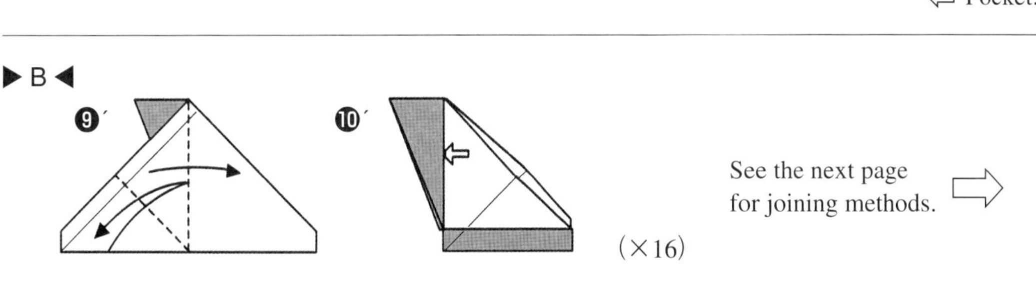


See the next page for joining methods. ⇨

## [Joining Method]

▶A◀

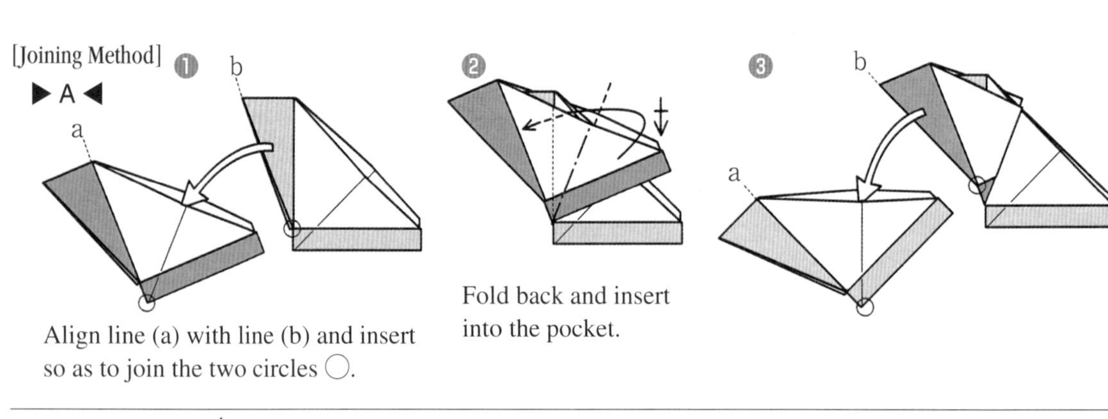


❶ Align line (a) with line (b) and insert so as to join the two circles ○.

❷ Fold back and insert into the pocket.

❸

❹ Join the 16 units in the same way.

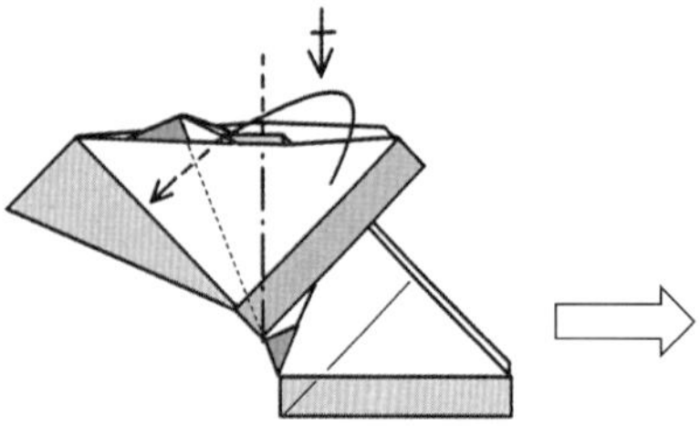

❺

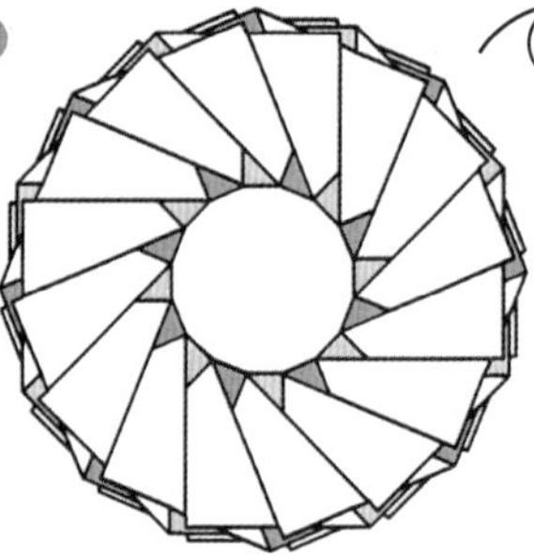

❻

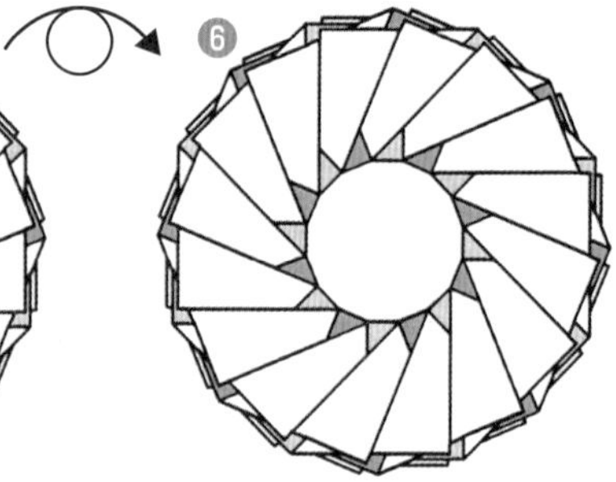

## [Joining Method]

▶B◀

❶

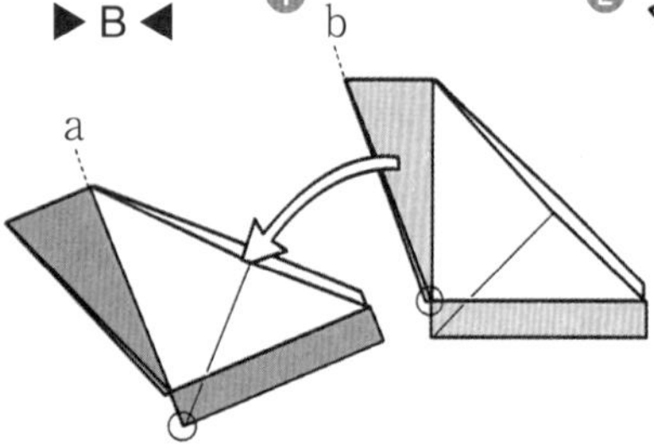

❷ Fold back the upper flap and insert into the pocket.

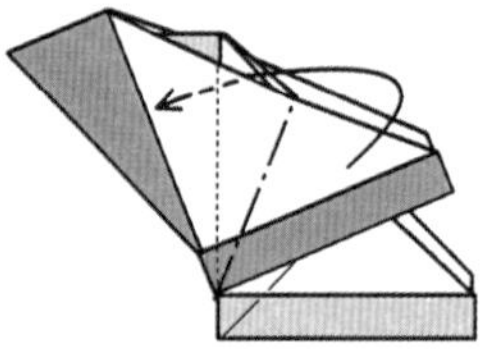

❸ Join in the same way as A.

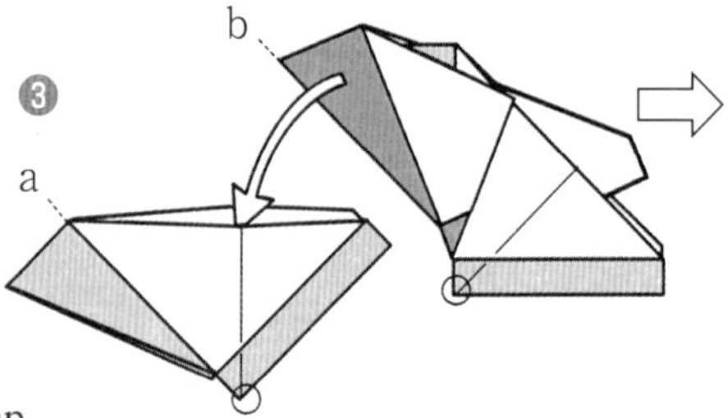

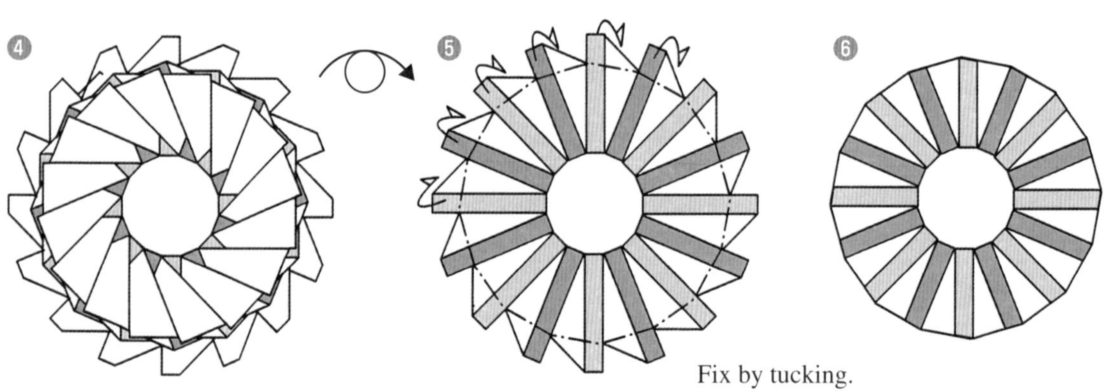

❹

❺

❻ Fix by tucking.

# RING 20

**Standard paper size:**
**7.5cm×7.5cm (3 in×3 in)**

This is the brother of Ring 19.
Use eight units.

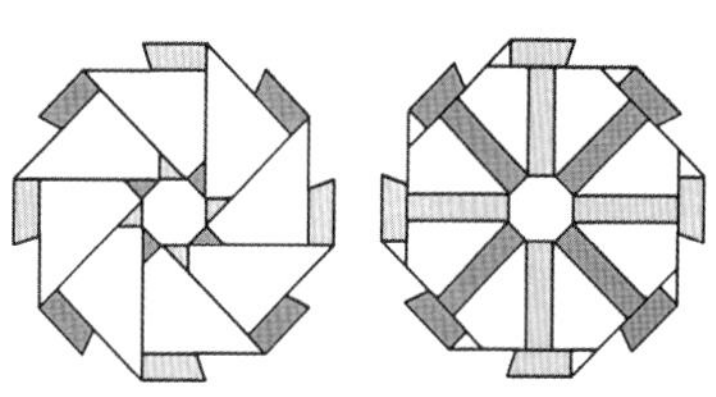

▶A◀

Starting from step ⓫ on page 77.

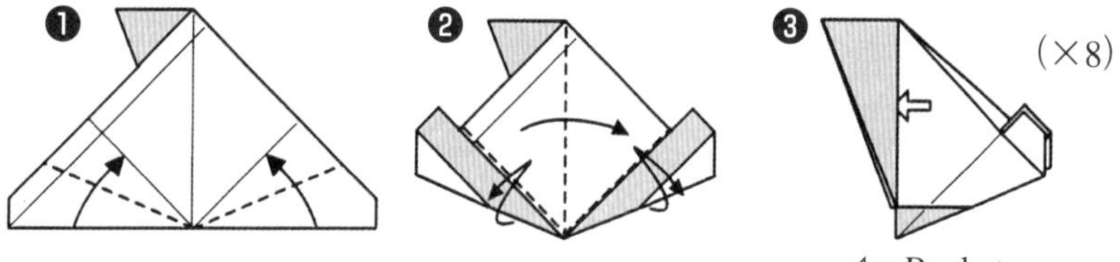

❶ ❷ ❸ (×8)

⇦ Pocket.

▶B◀

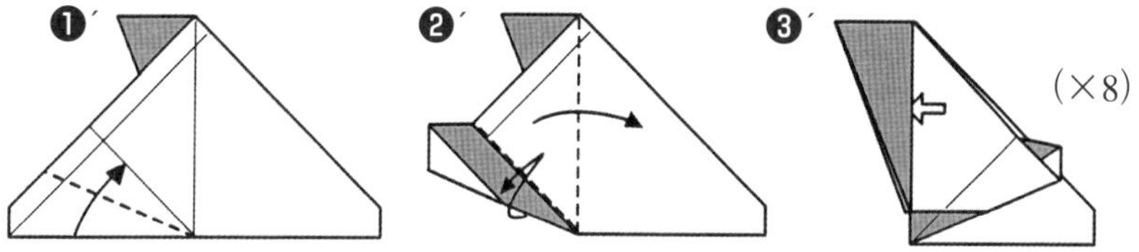

❶′ ❷′ ❸′ (×8)

▶C◀

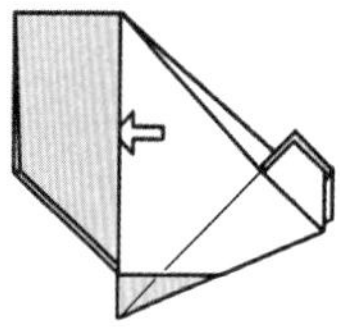

You may fold the bottom like this.

[Joining Method]

▶A◀

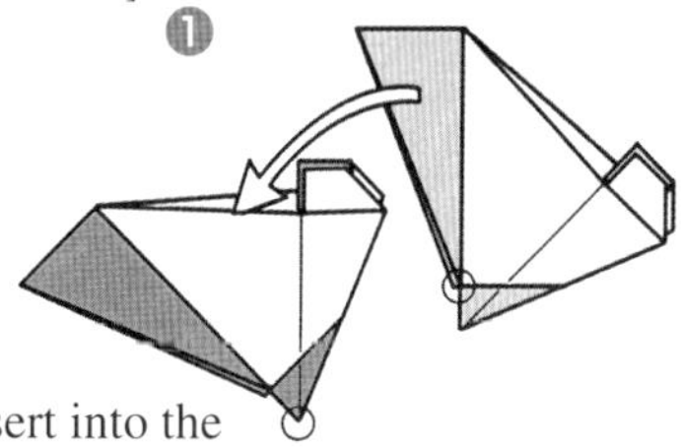

❶ Insert into the pocket by joining the circles ○.

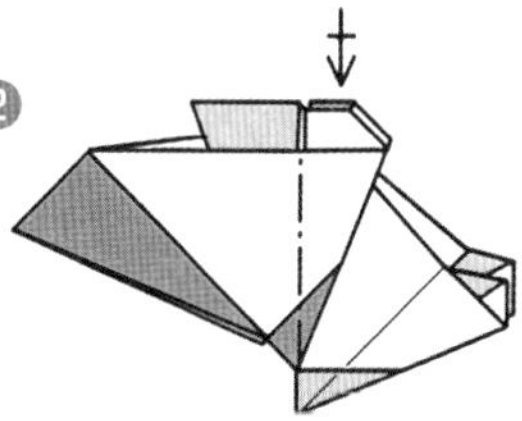

❷ Fold back and tuck.

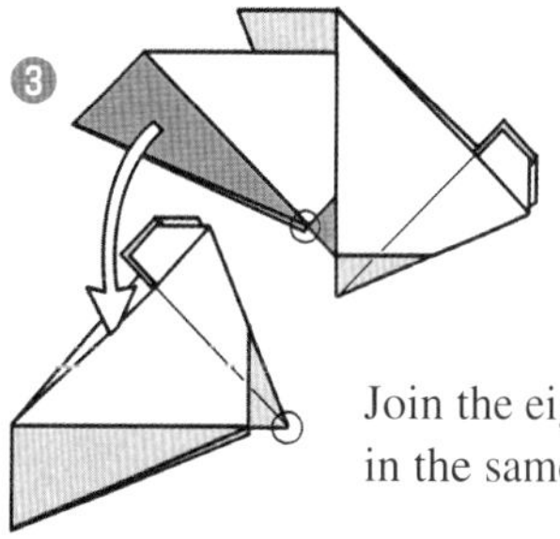

❸ Join the eight units in the same way.

▶A◀

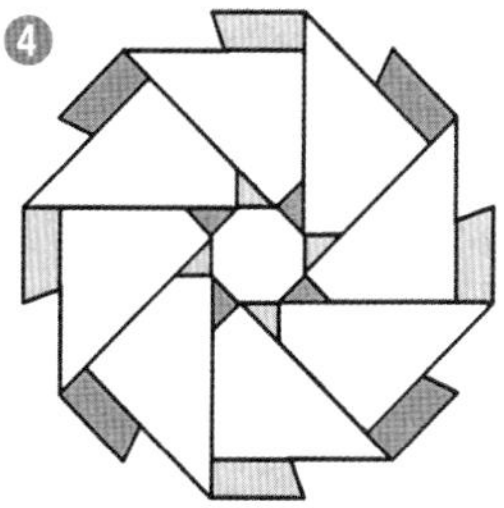

❹ The back side has the same patterns.

▶B◀

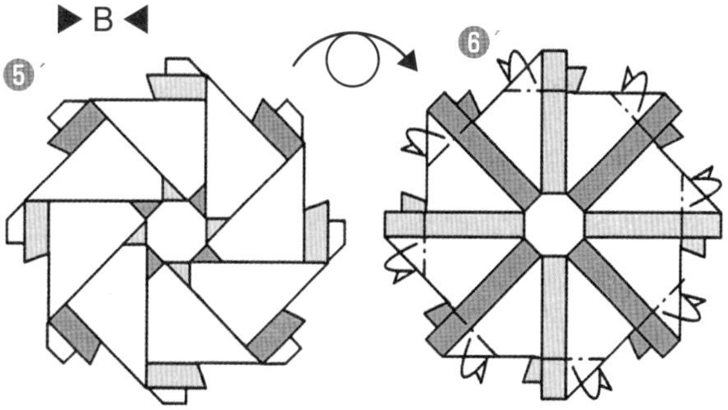

❺′ ❻′ ❼′

The front side is joined in the same way as A and fold the back side as shown.

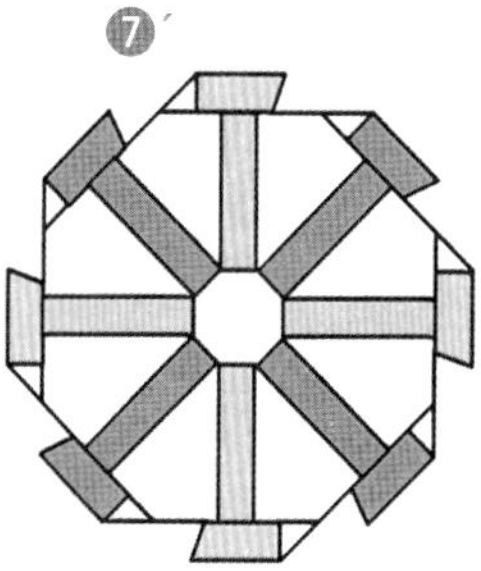

# RING 21

Standard paper size:
7.5cm×7.5cm (3 in×3 in)

The basic method is the same as that of Ring 19. Use 16 units. It is possible to change the folding position like A′.

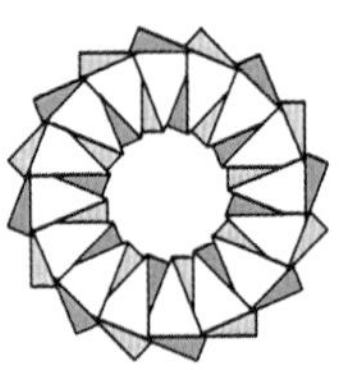

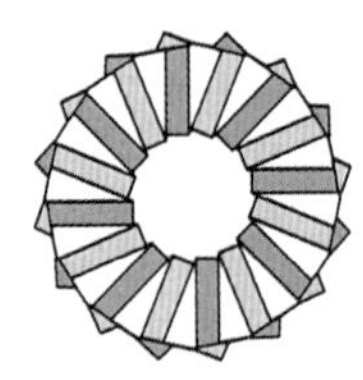

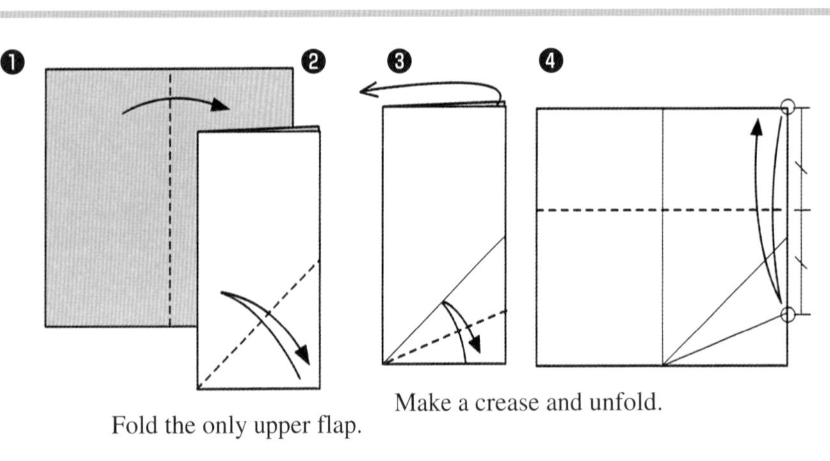


Fold the only upper flap.

Make a crease and unfold.

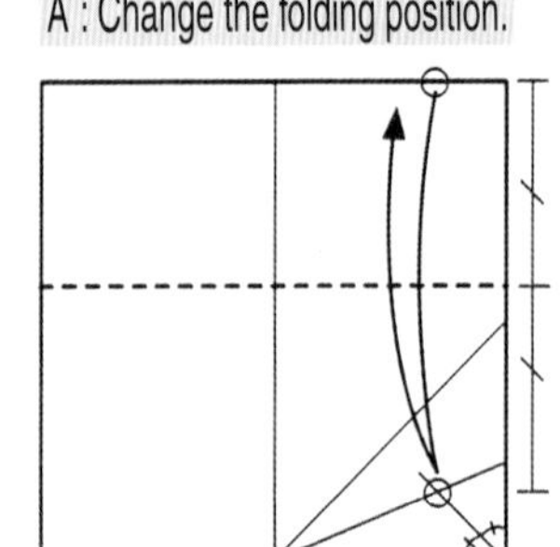


The completed shape becomes a little different.

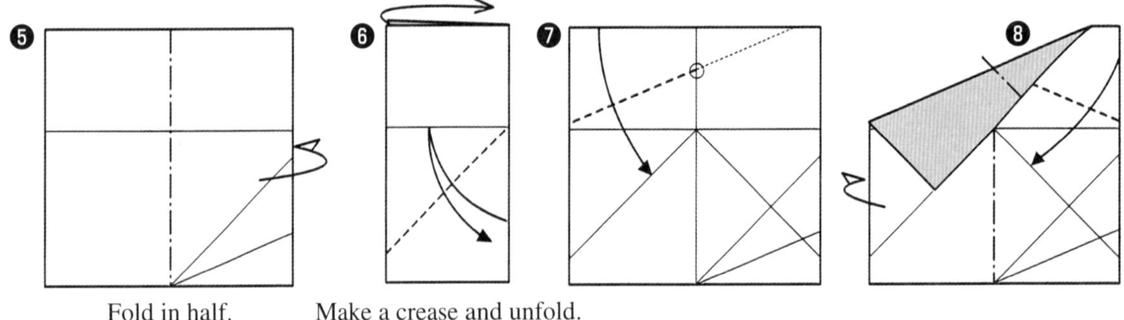


Fold in half.

Make a crease and unfold.

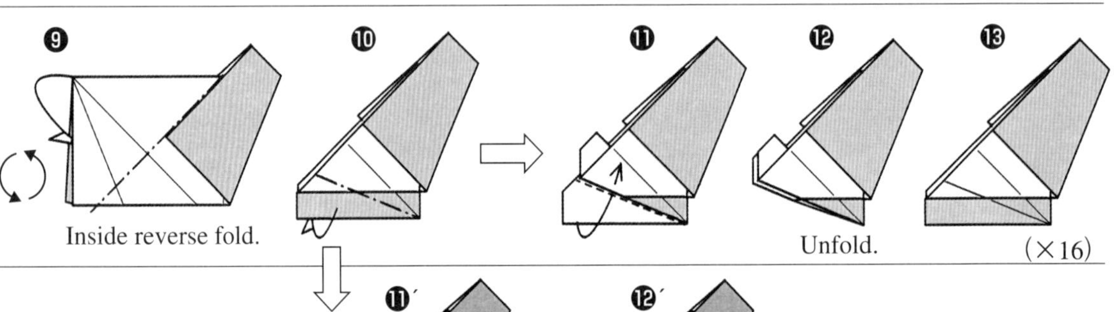


Inside reverse fold.

Unfold.

(×16)

⓫′ ⓬′

▶B◀

Unfold.

(×16)

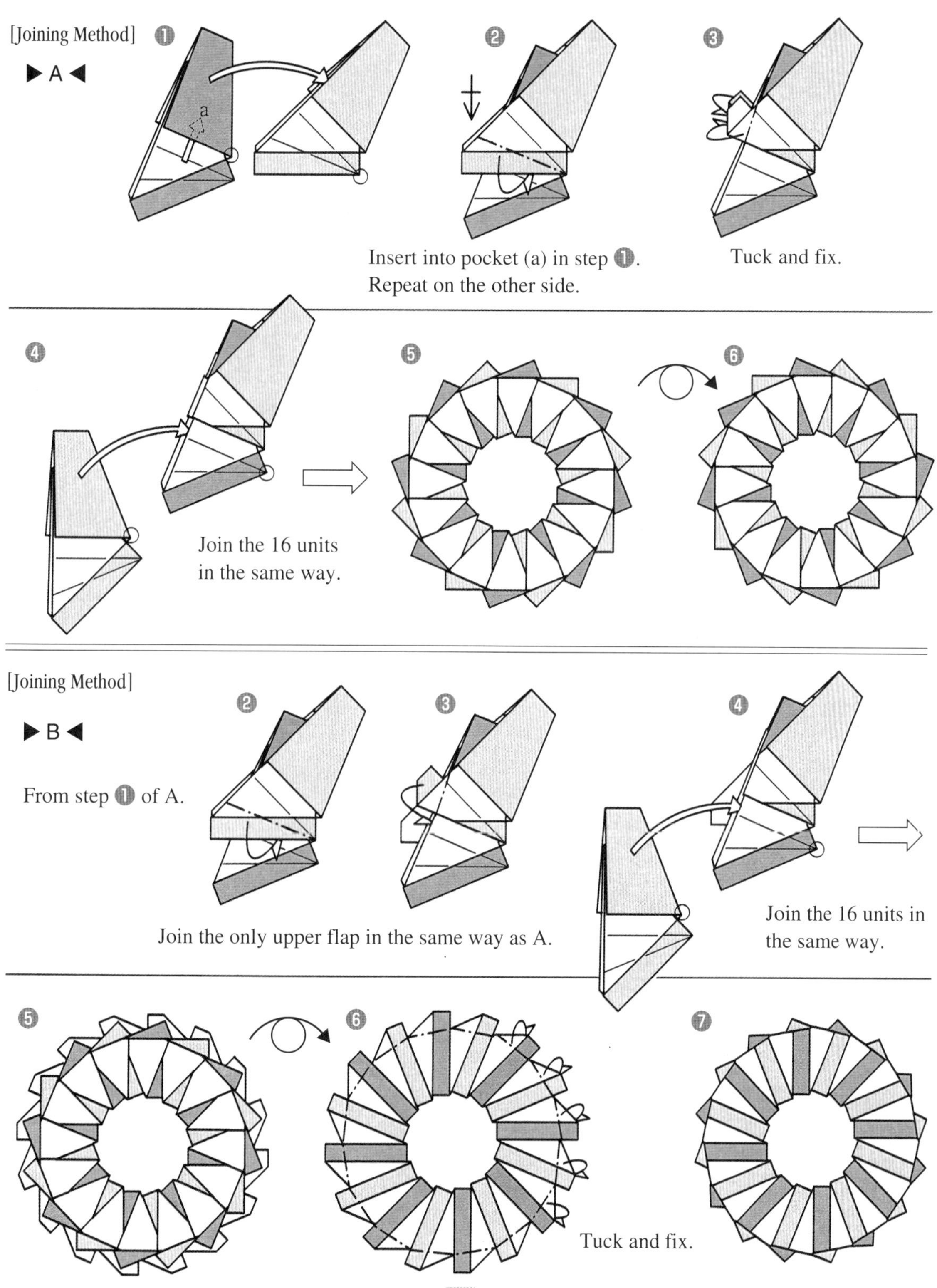
[Joining Method]
▶ A ◀
❶
a
❷
❸
Insert into pocket (a) in step ❶.
Repeat on the other side.
Tuck and fix.
❹
❺
❻
Join the 16 units
in the same way.
[Joining Method]
▶ B ◀
From step ❶ of A.
❷
❸
❹
Join the only upper flap in the same way as A.
Join the 16 units in
the same way.
❺
❻
❼
Tuck and fix.

# RING 22

Standard paper size:
7.5cm×7.5cm (3 in×3 in)

Basically this ring is the same as Ring 19 on page 77, but the center hole is a bit larger.

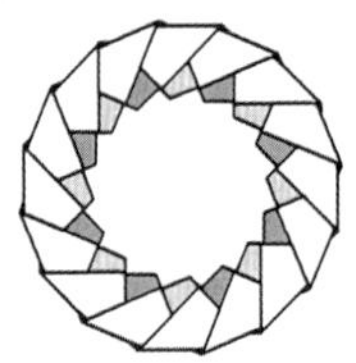

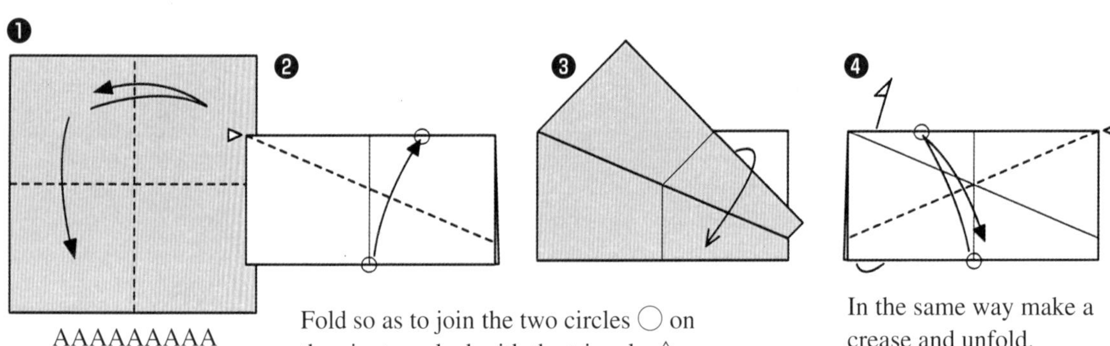

AAAAAAAAA

Fold so as to join the two circles ○ on the pivot marked with the triangle △.

In the same way make a crease and unfold.

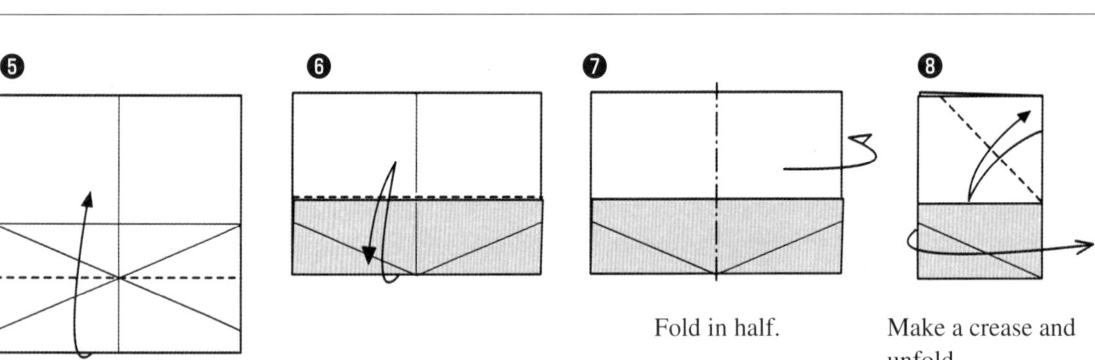

Fold in half.

Make a crease and unfold.

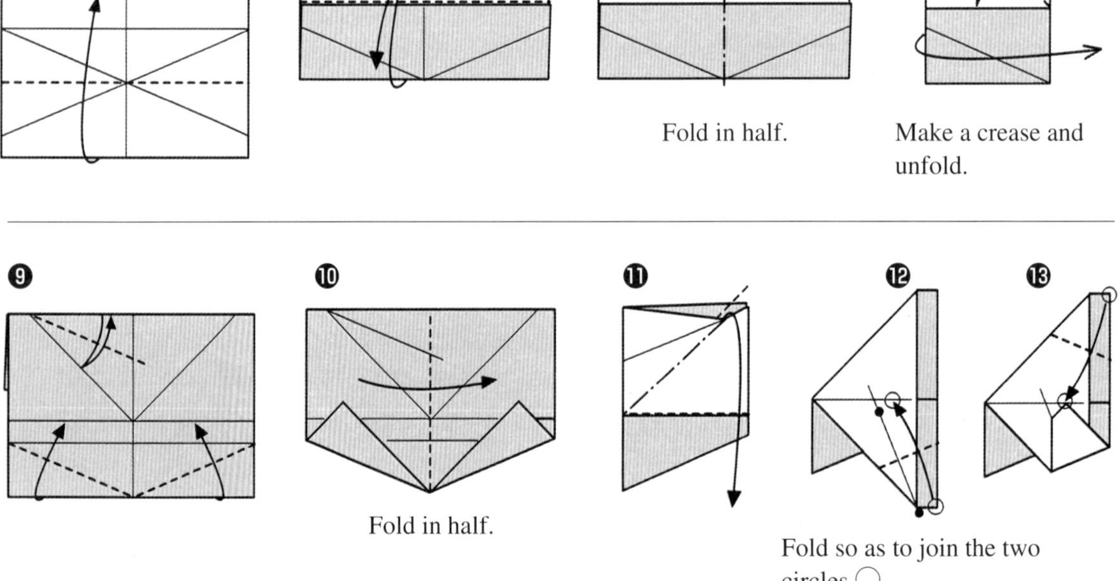

Fold in half.

Fold so as to join the two circles ○.

Continued on the next page.

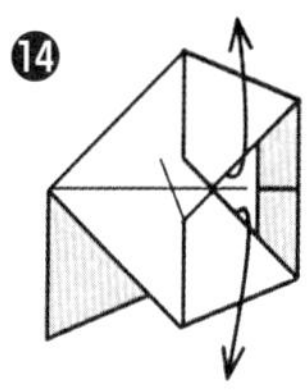

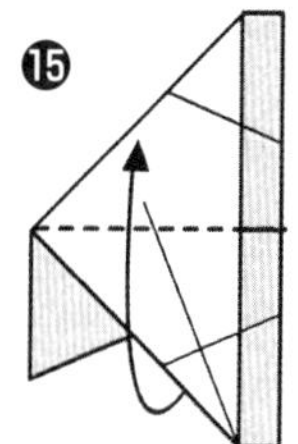

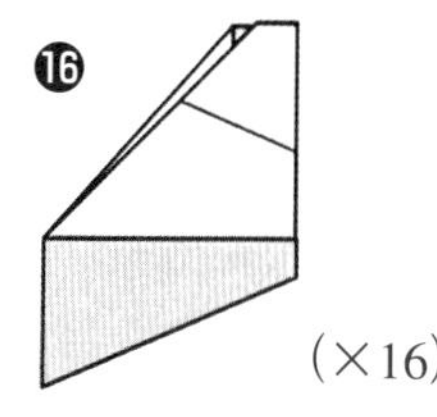

(×16)

[Joining Method]

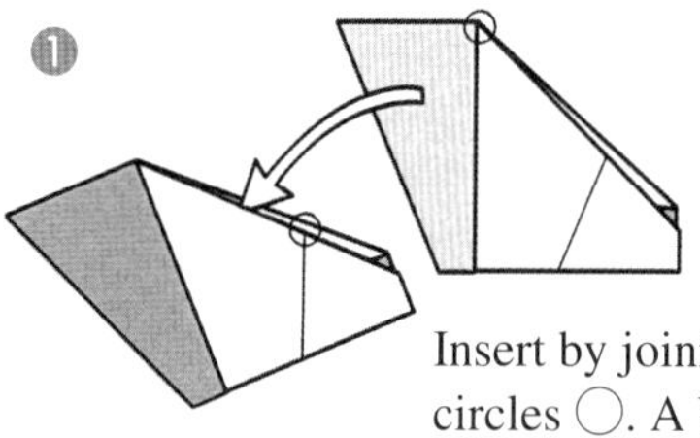

Insert by joining the two circles ◯. A bit of top will appear because of the thickness of the paper.

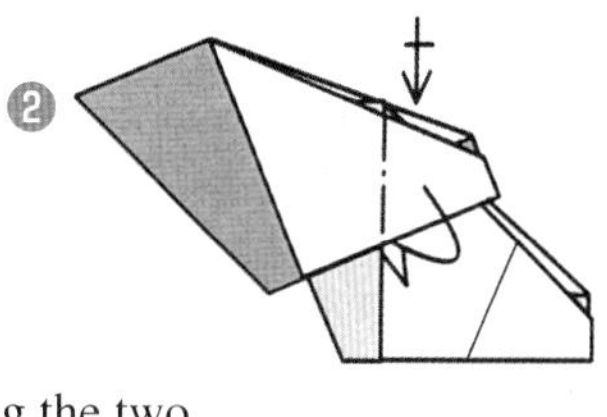

Tuck into the pocket. Repeat on the other side.

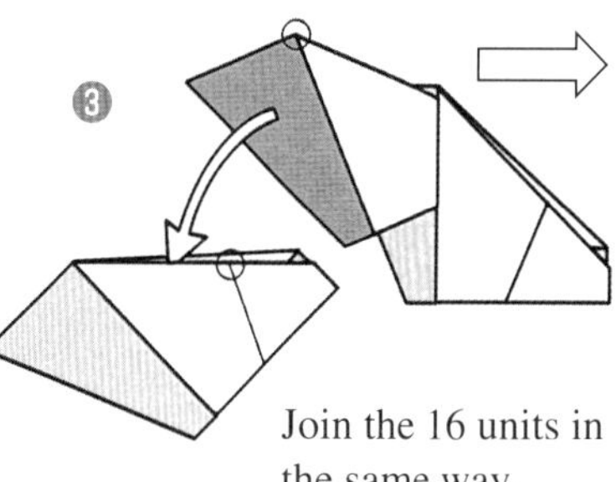

Join the 16 units in the same way.

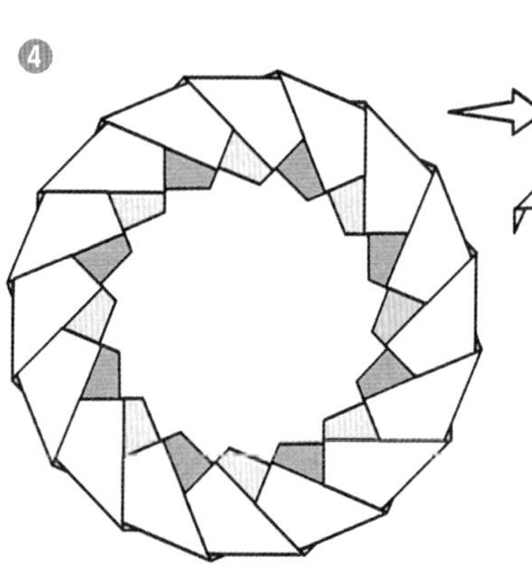

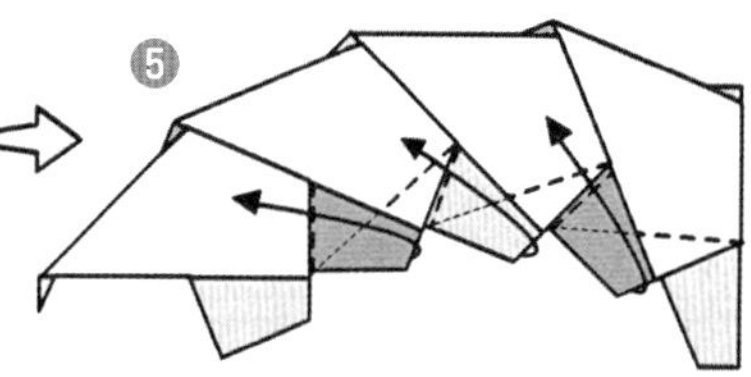

Fold by opening the small flap.

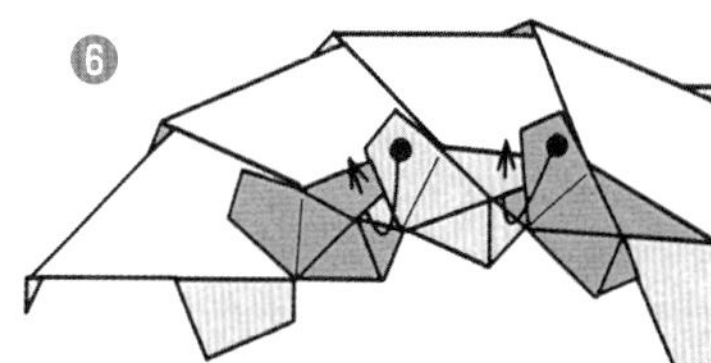

Put the tip into the pocket.

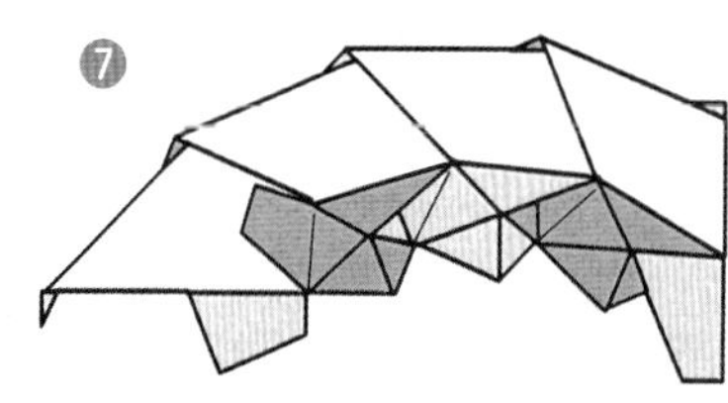

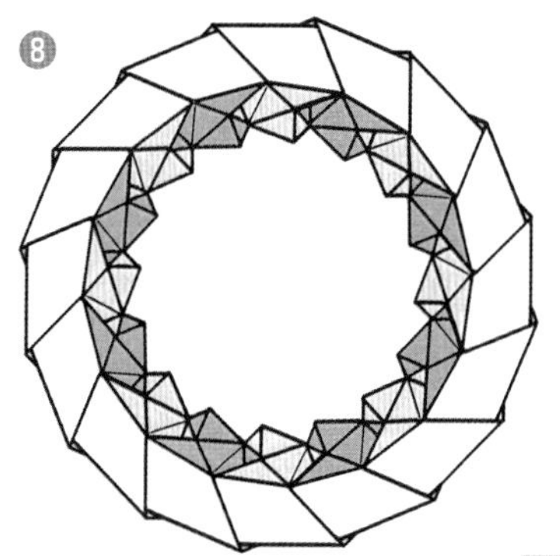

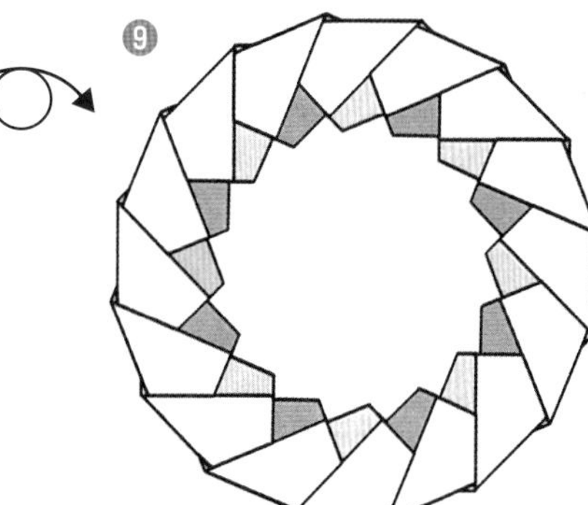

# RING 23

Standard paper size:
7.5cm×7.5cm (3 in×3 in)

The angles of the ring of 20 units have a play but the ring is joined nicely.

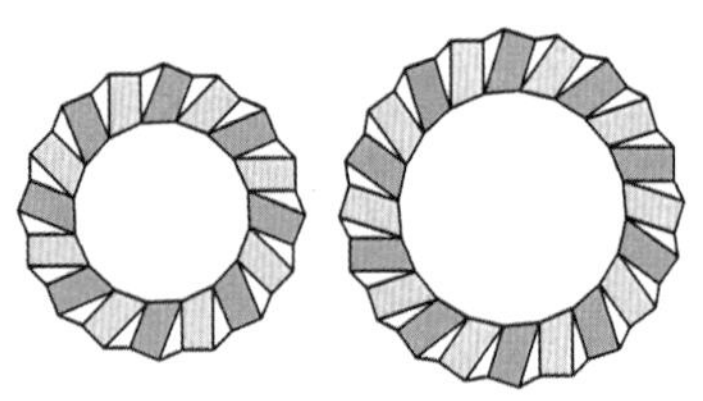

▶ 16 units ◀

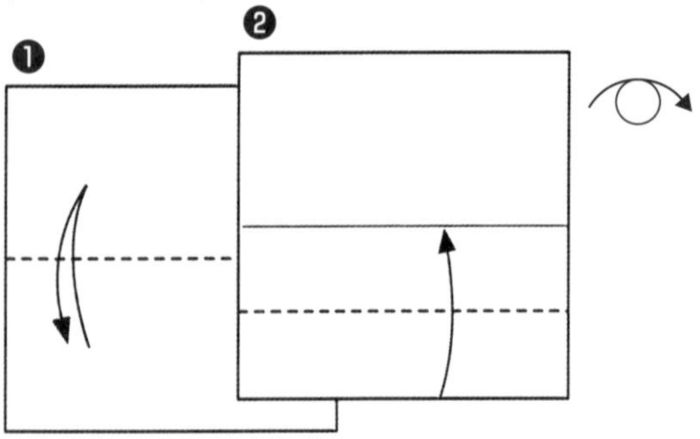

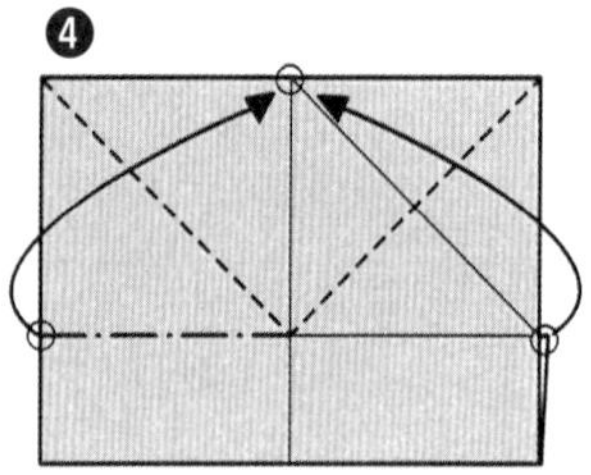

❶ ❷ ❸ ❹

Fold together according to creases.

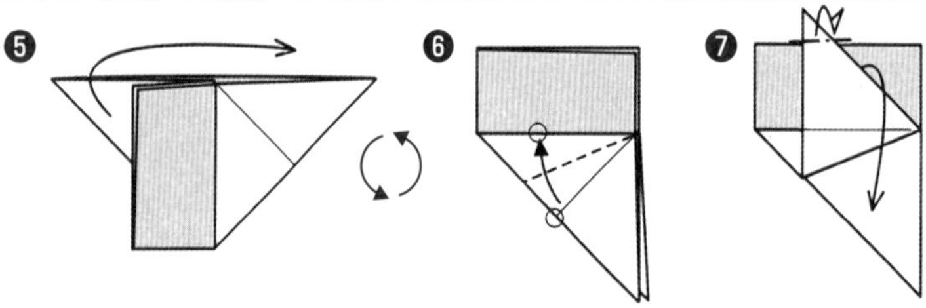

❺ ❻ ❼

Fold along the side.

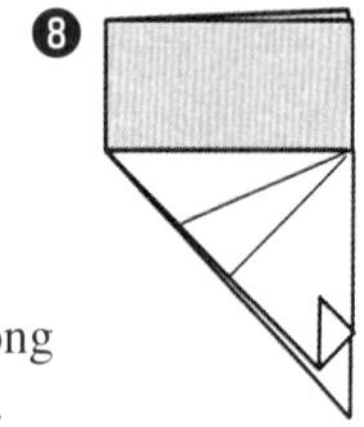

❽

(×16)

[Joining Method]

❶

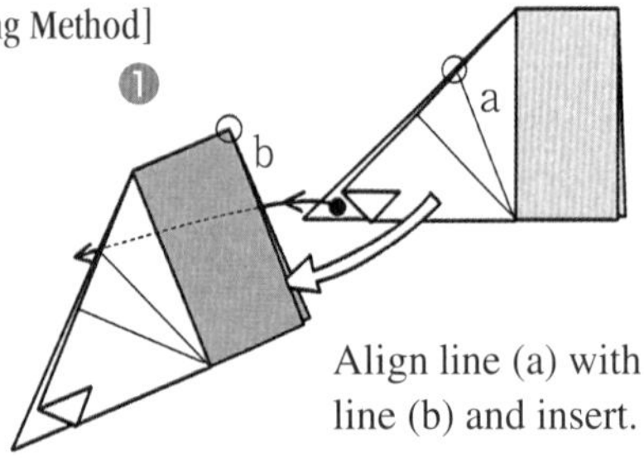

Align line (a) with line (b) and insert.

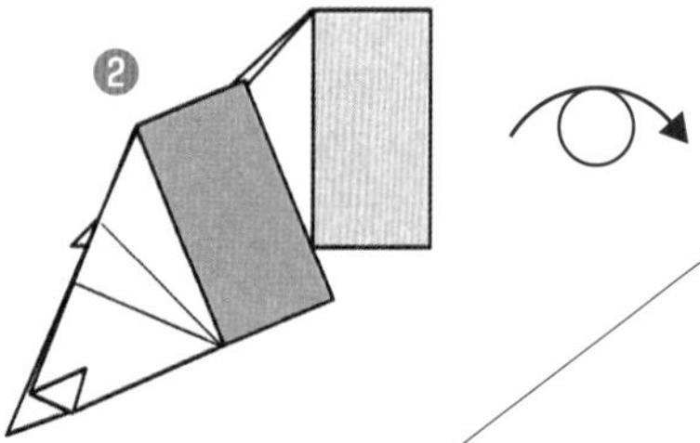

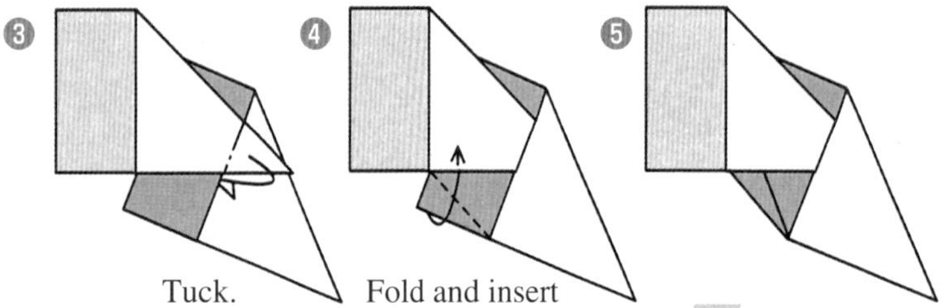

❷

❸ Tuck.

❹ Fold and insert into the pocket.

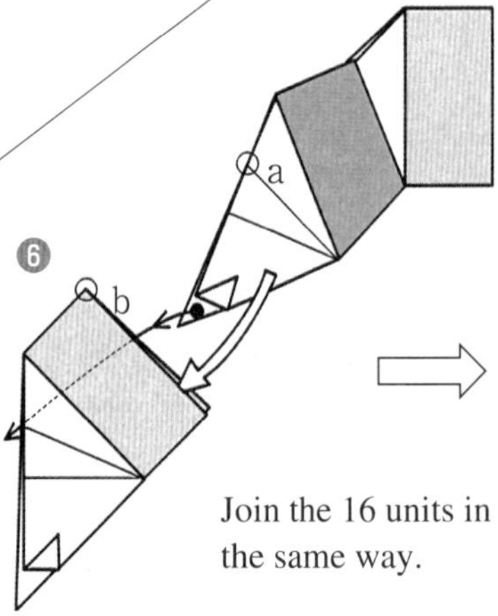

❺

❻

Join the 16 units in the same way.

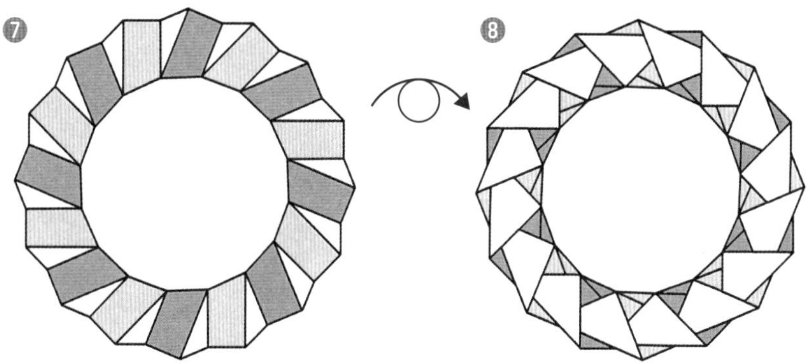

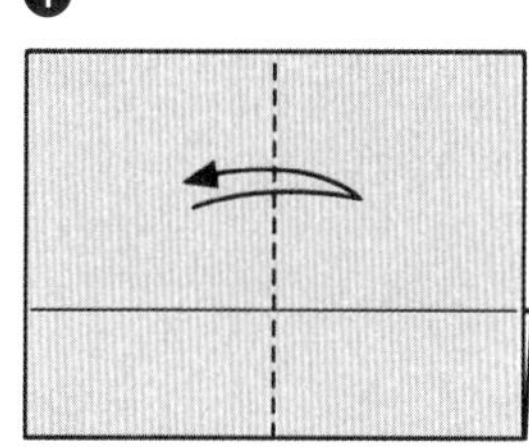

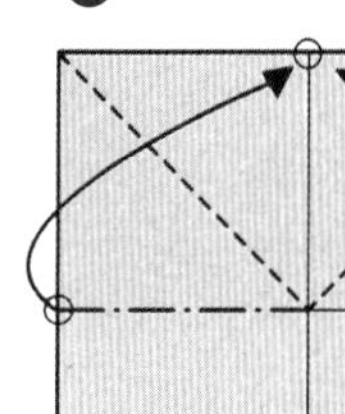

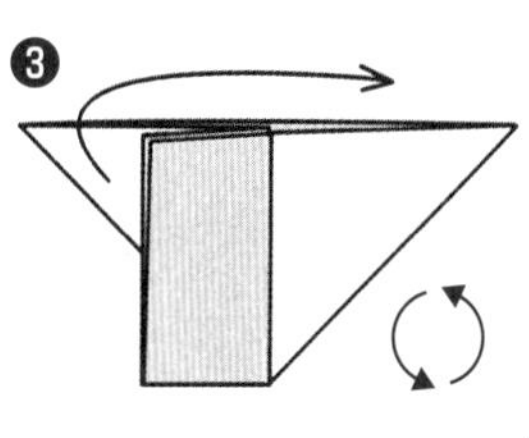

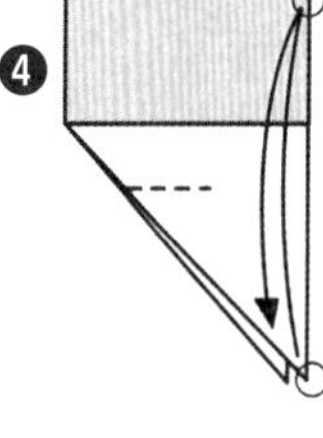

Make a bit of crease on the upper flap.

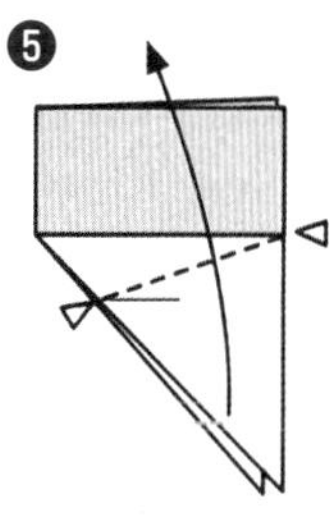

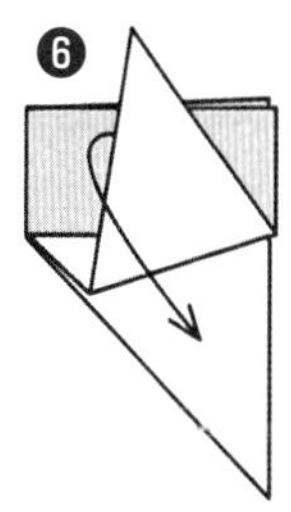

(×20)

[Joining Method]

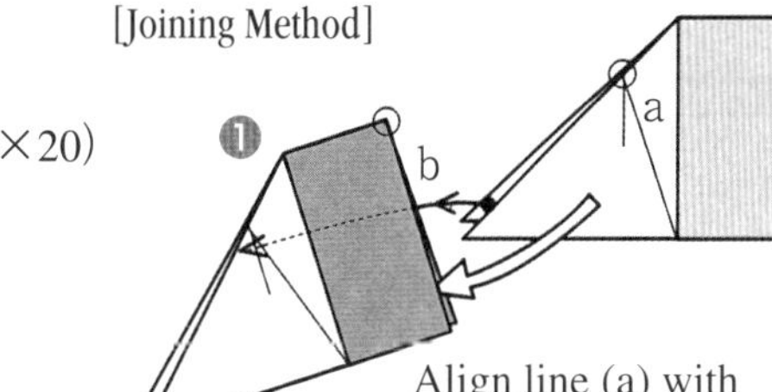


Align line (a) with line (b) and insert.

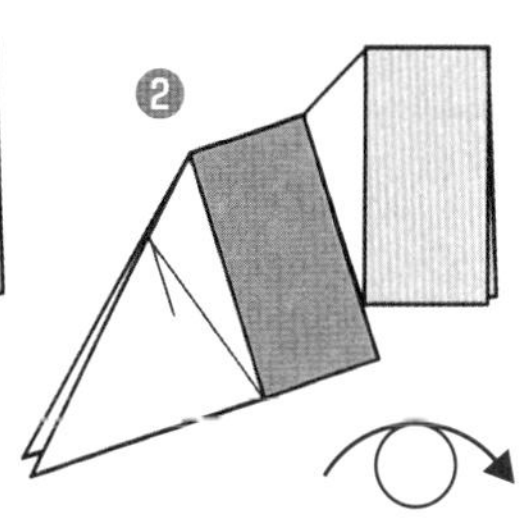

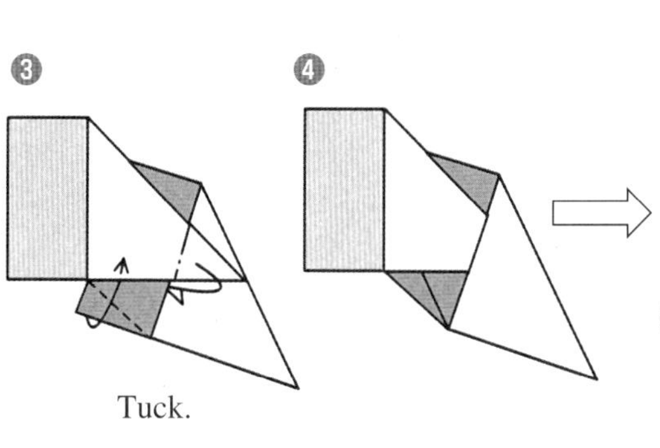

Tuck.

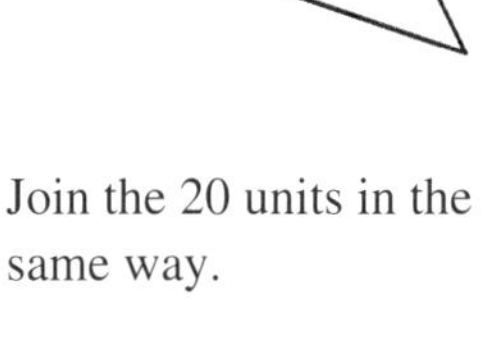

Join the 20 units in the same way.

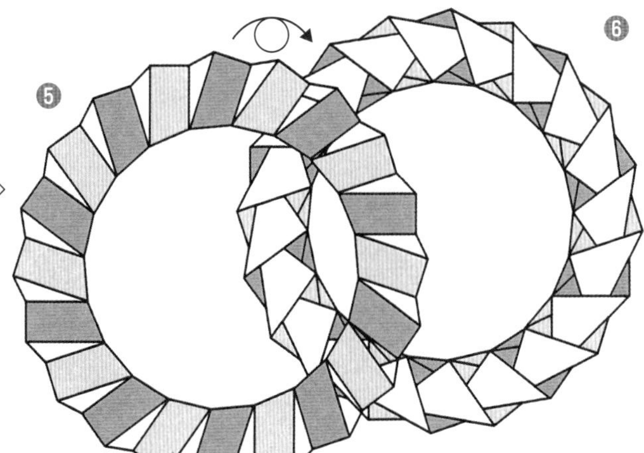

# RING 24

Standard paper size:
7.5cm×7.5cm (3 in×3 in)

A gorgeous ring like flowers.
If you fold the tips like B,
it is also nice.

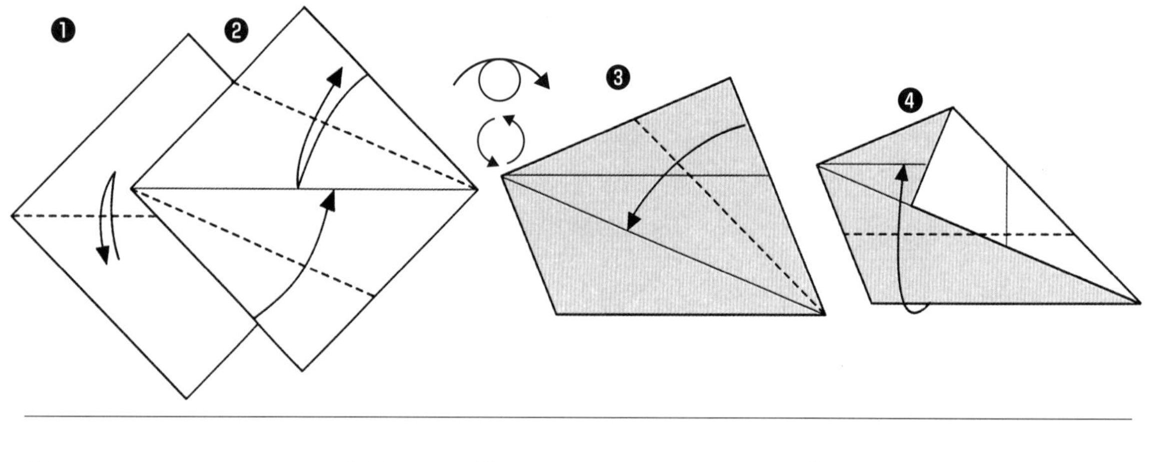

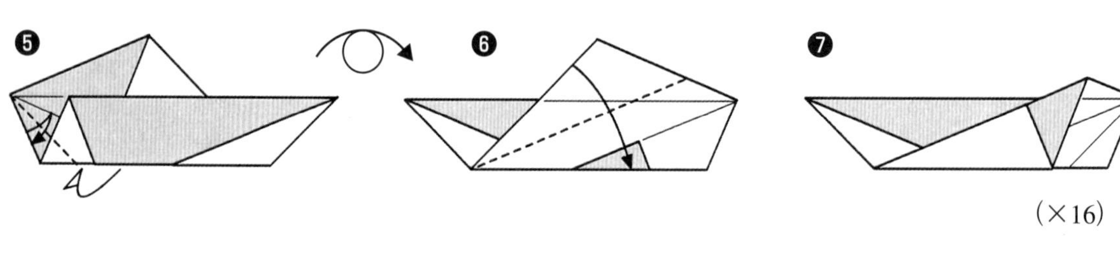

(×16)

[Joining Method]

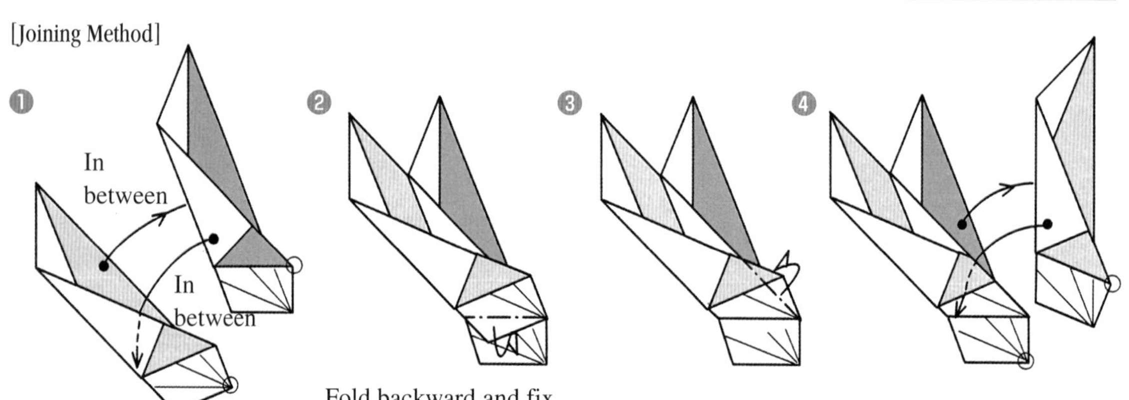


❶ Insert by joining the two circles ○.

❷ Fold backward and fix. (Fold back on the crease made in step ❺.)

❸ Fold backward and fix.

❹ Insert by joining the two circles ○.

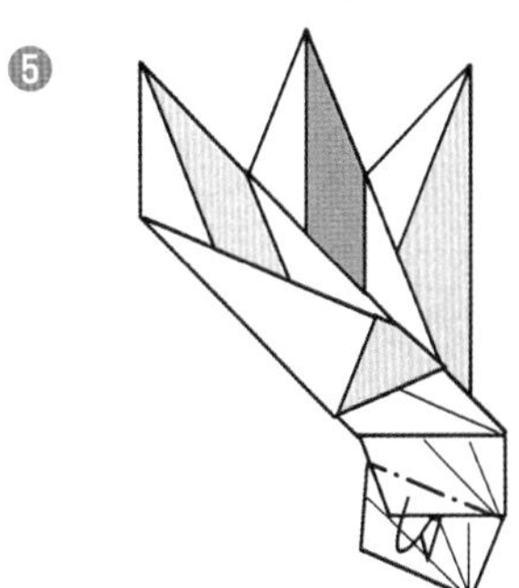

Fold backward and fix.

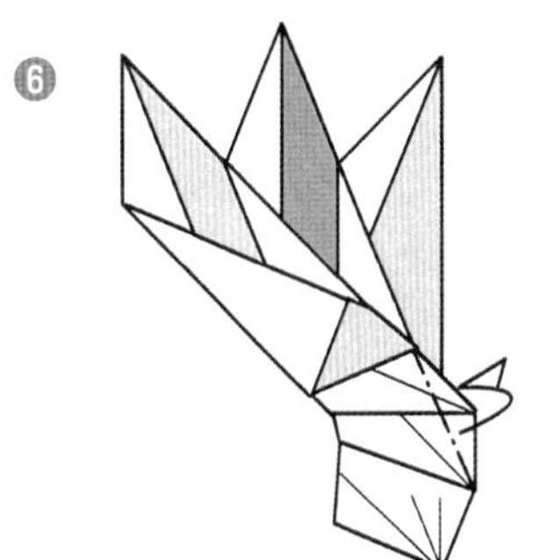

Fold backward and fix.

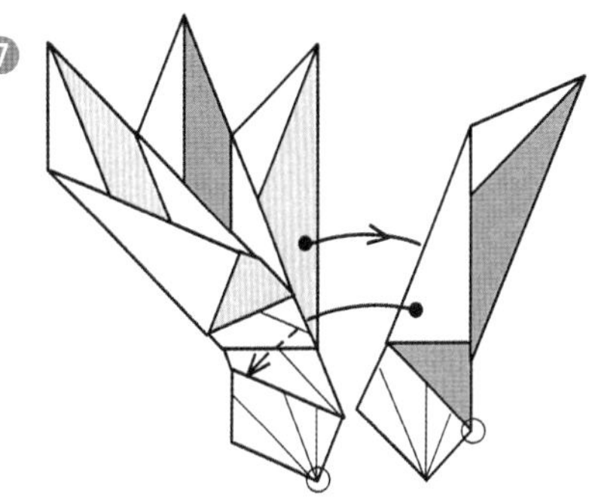

Insert by joining the two circles ○.

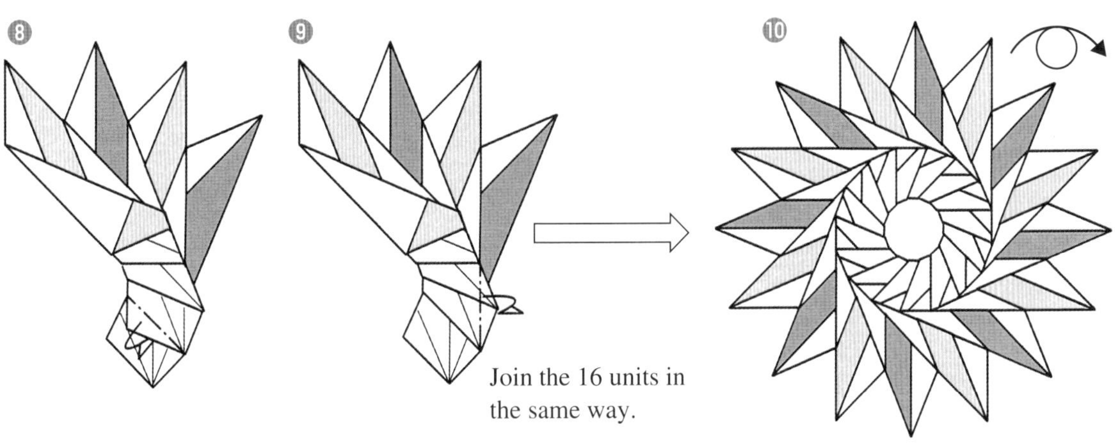

Join the 16 units in the same way.

▶A◀

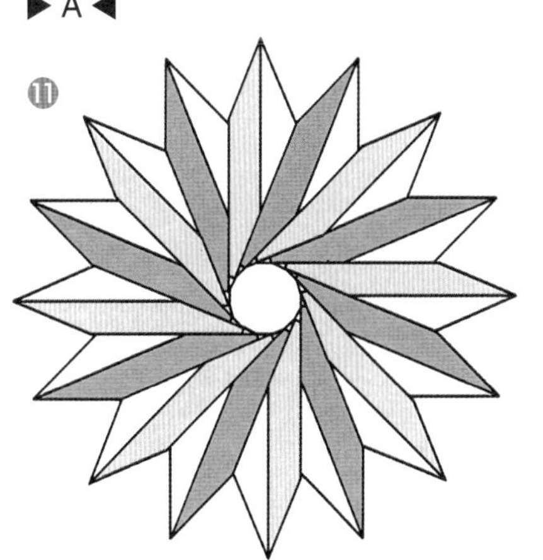

▶B◀

Fold the tip and insert into the pocket.

# RING 25

Standard paper size:
7.5cm×7.5cm (3 in×3 in)

This is the brother of Ring 24 with larger hole than that.

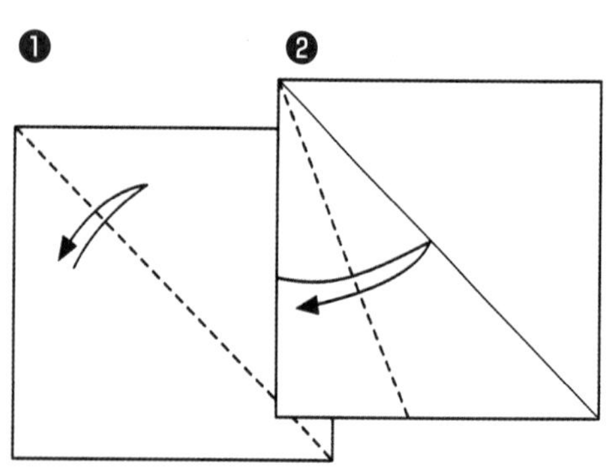

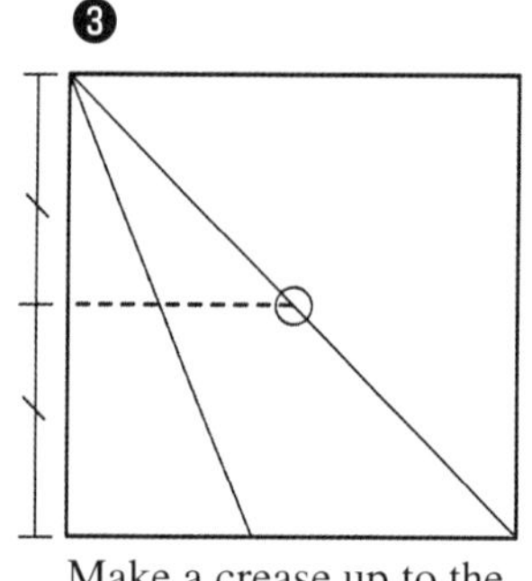

Make a crease up to the point ○.

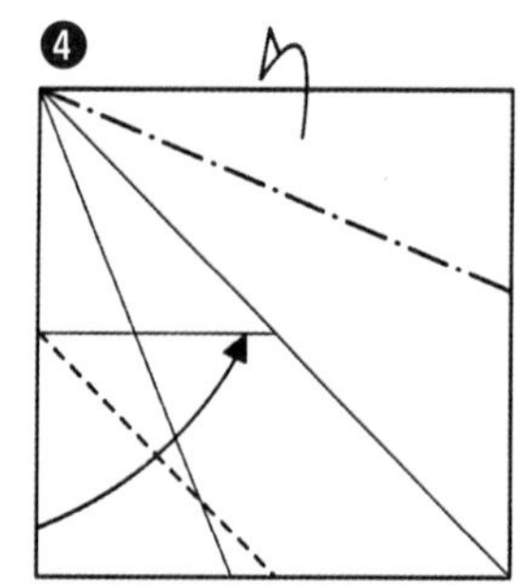

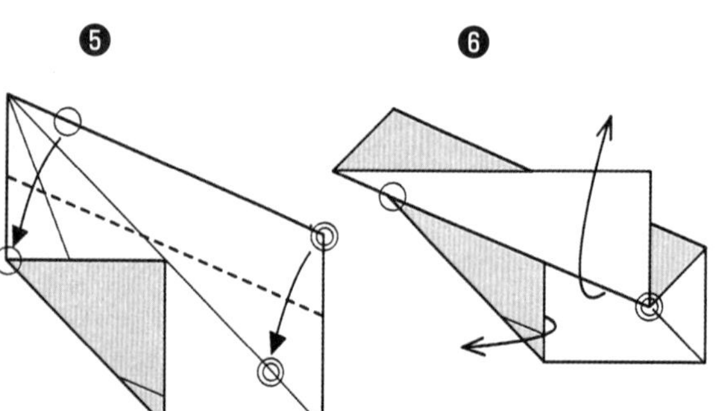

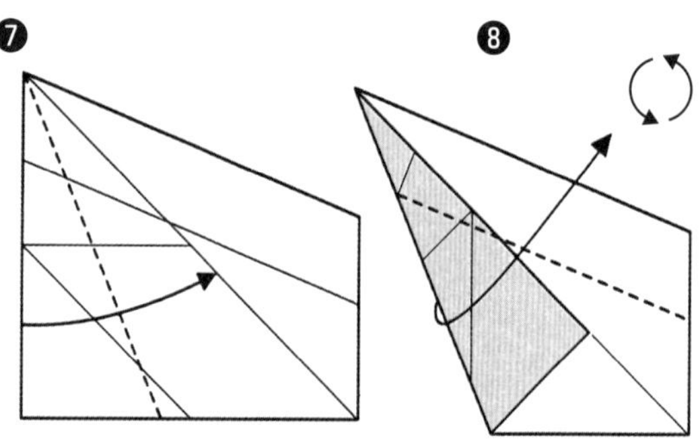

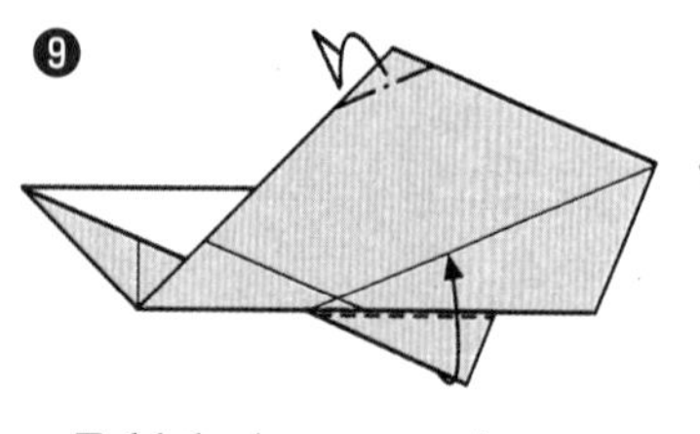

Fold the bottom as shown.

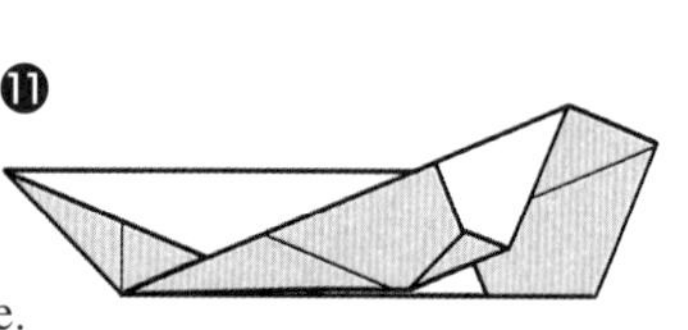

Fold back the top on the crease.

[Joining Method]

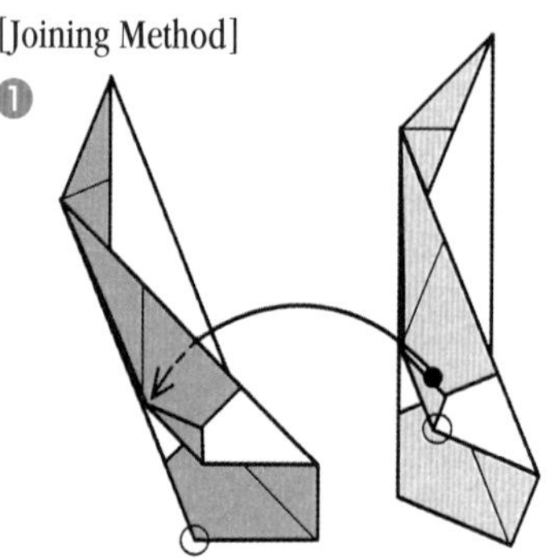

Insert so as to join the two circles ○.

(×16)

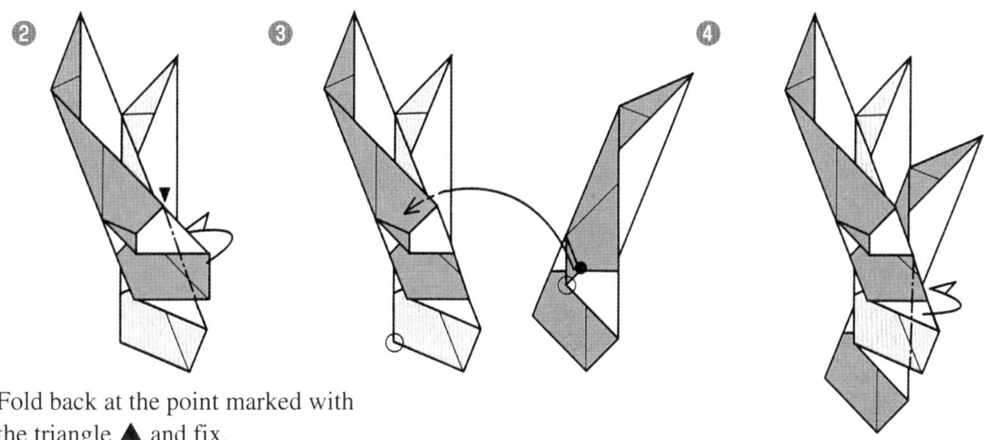


Fold back at the point marked with the triangle ▲ and fix.

Join the 16 units in the same way.

▶B◀

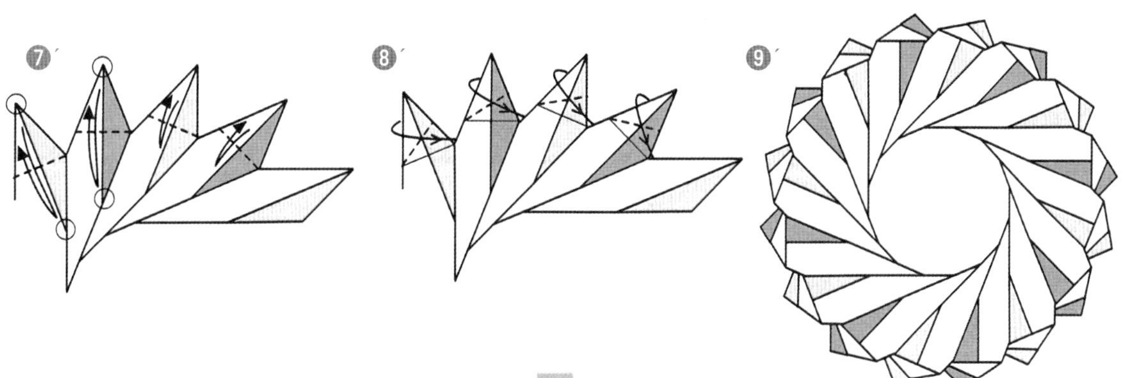

# RING 26

Standard paper size:
7.5cm×7.5cm (3 in×3 in)

A sturdy ring locked firmly.

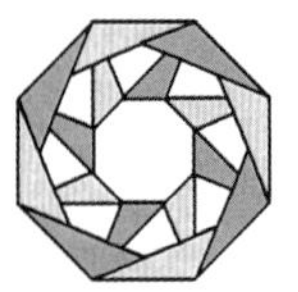

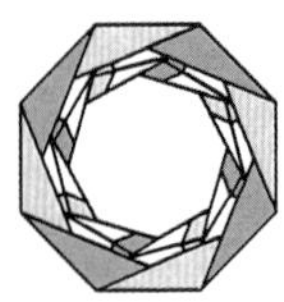

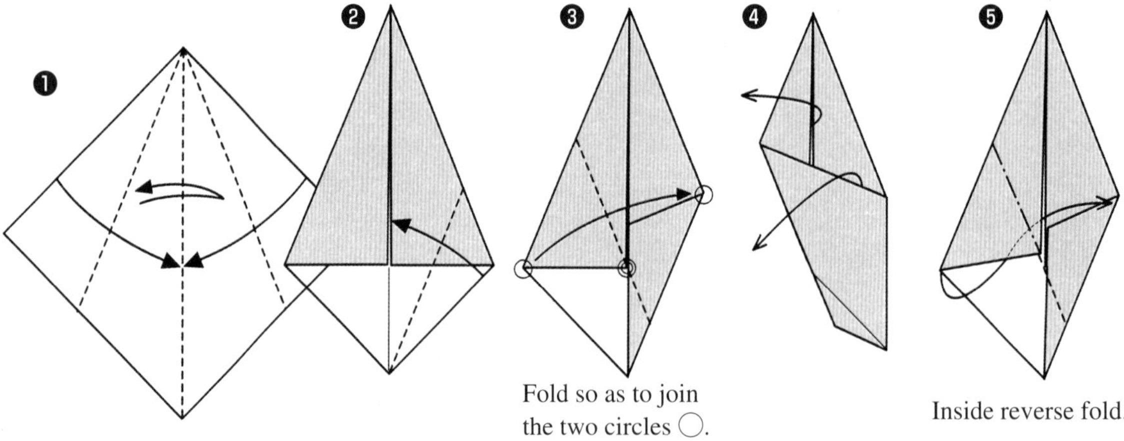

❶

❷

❸

Fold so as to join the two circles ○.

❹

❺

Inside reverse fold.

▶A◀

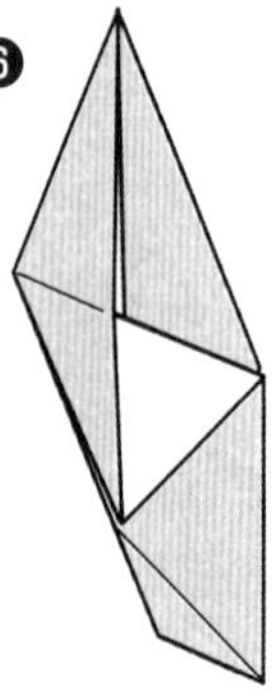

❻

(×8)

[Joining Method of A]

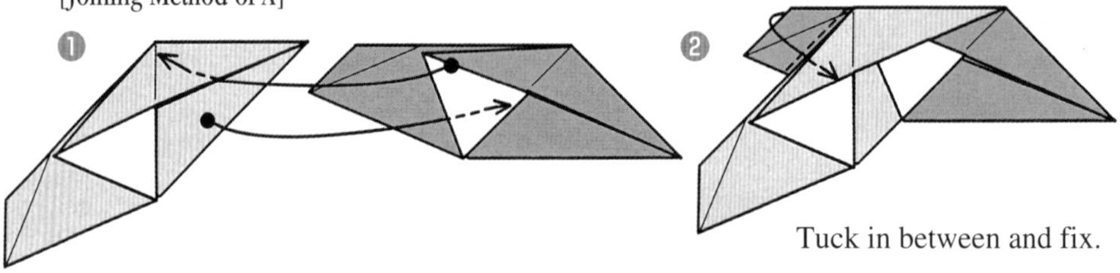

❶

❷

Tuck in between and fix.

❸

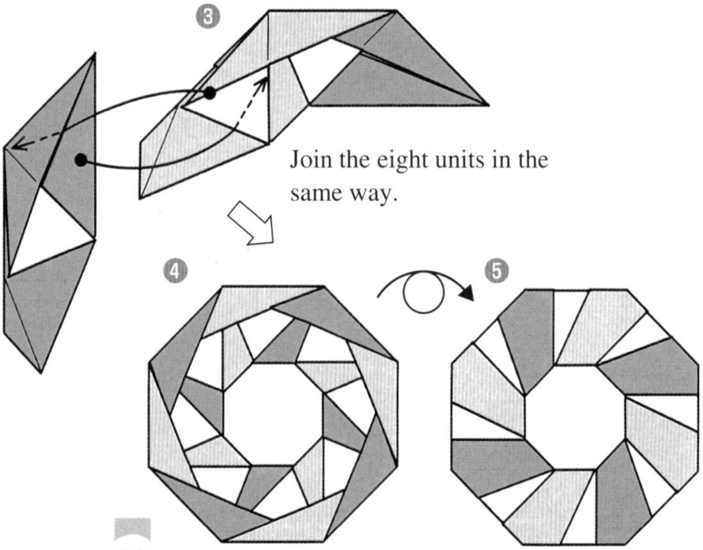

Join the eight units in the same way.

❹

❺

▶B◀

❼

❽

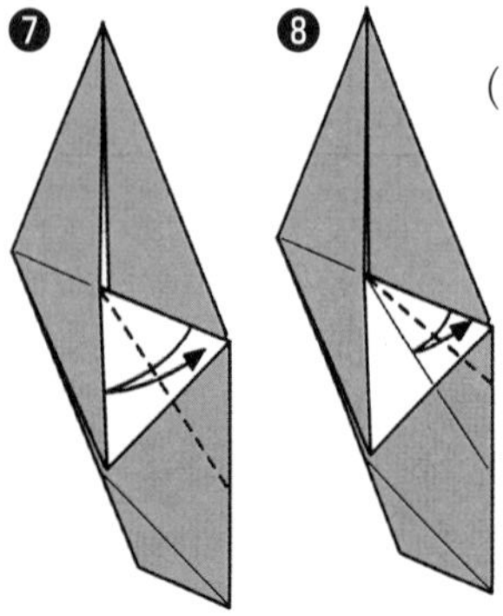

(×8)

[Joining Method of B]

Starting from step ❷ of Joining Method of A.

❷

Fold on the line made in ❽.

❸

Join the eight units in the same way.

❹

❺

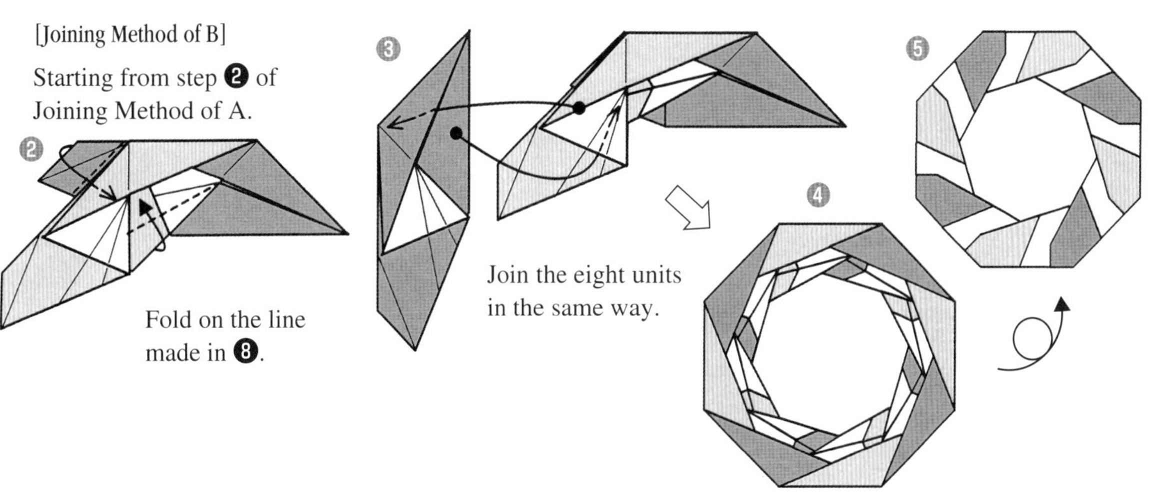

# RING 27

**Standard paper size: 7.5cm×7.5cm (3 in×3 in)**

The methods of folding and joining are very simple.

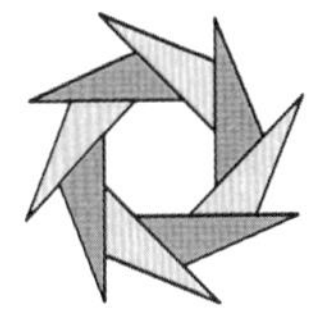

❶

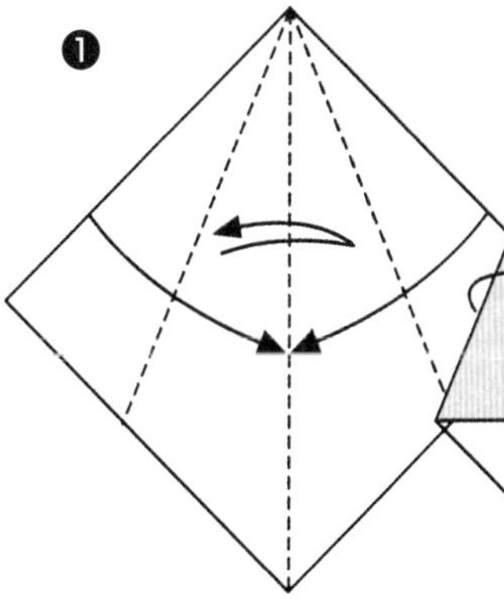

❷

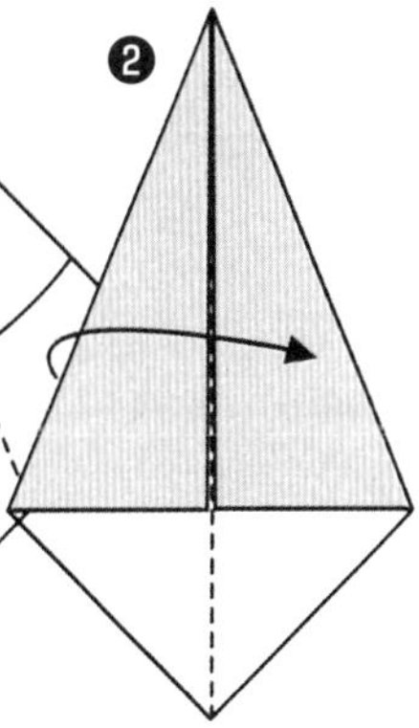

❸

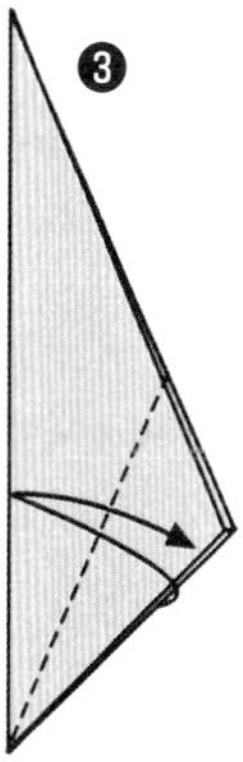

[Joining Method] ➊

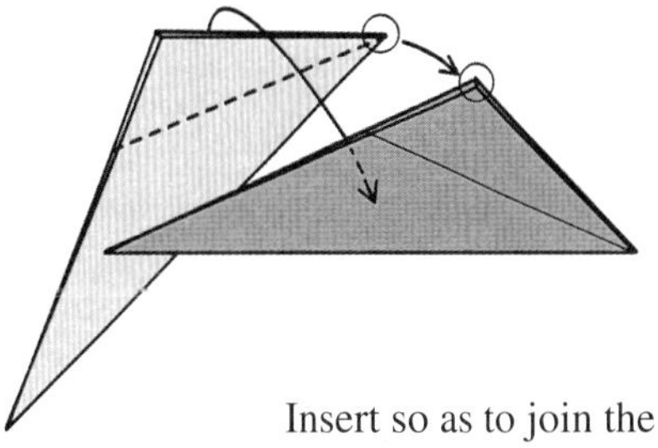

Insert so as to join the two circles ○.

(×8)

❷

❸

Join the eight units in the same way.

❹

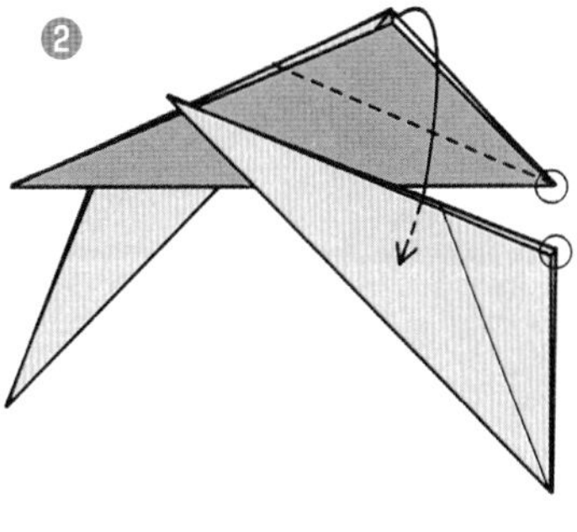

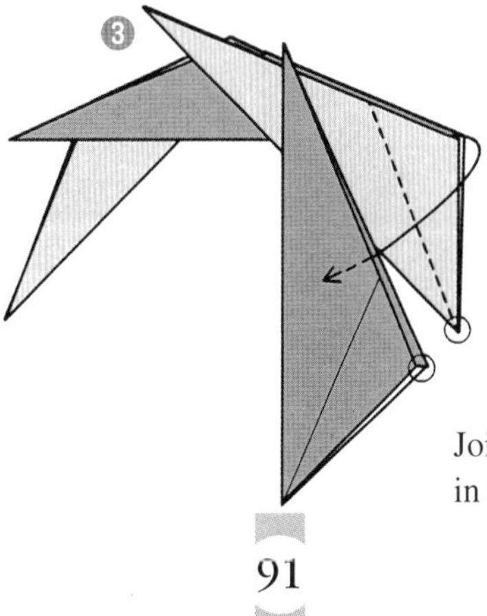

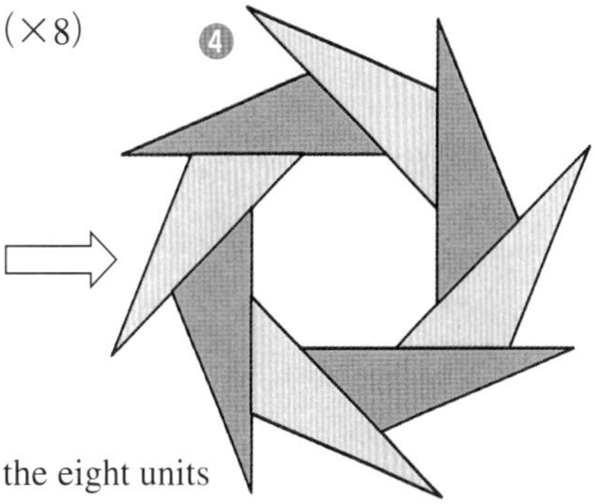

# RING 28

Standard paper size:
7.5cm×7.5cm (3 in×3 in)

You can make three kinds of rings by making a bit of changes in folding. Use 16 units.

❶

❷

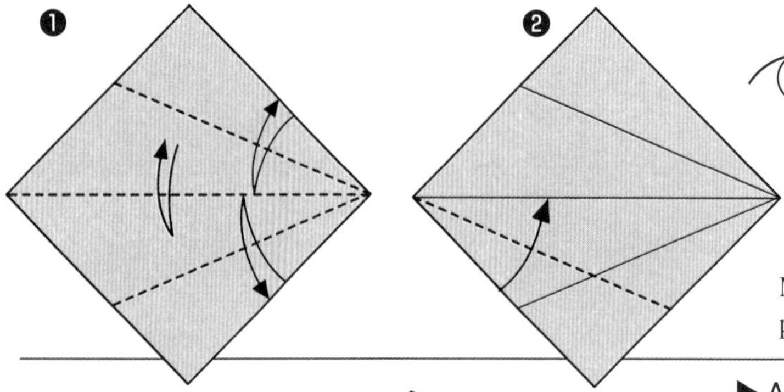

❸

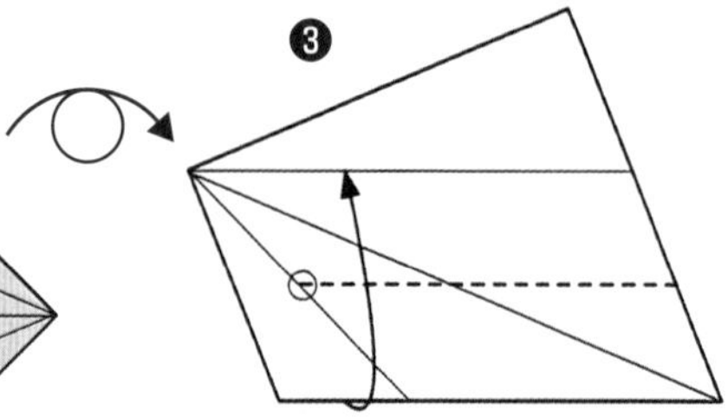

Make a crease by folding up to the point marked with the circle ○.

❹

❺

▶A◀

❻

❼ (×16)

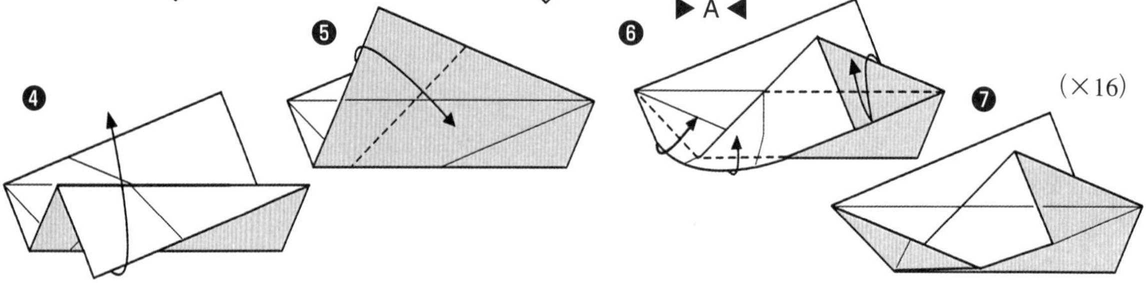

▶B◀

❻′

❼′

❽′

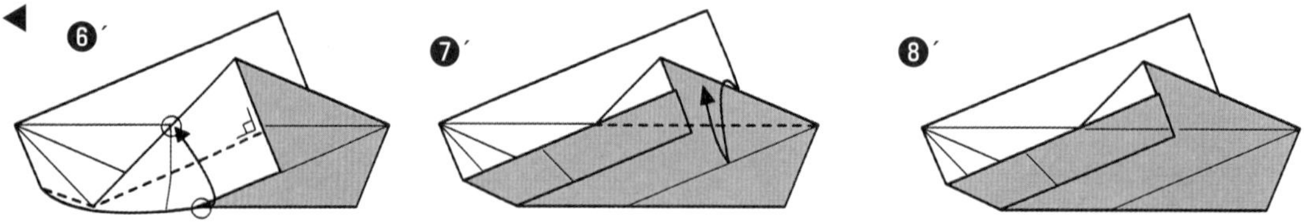

▶C◀

Turn over ❷.

❸″

❹″

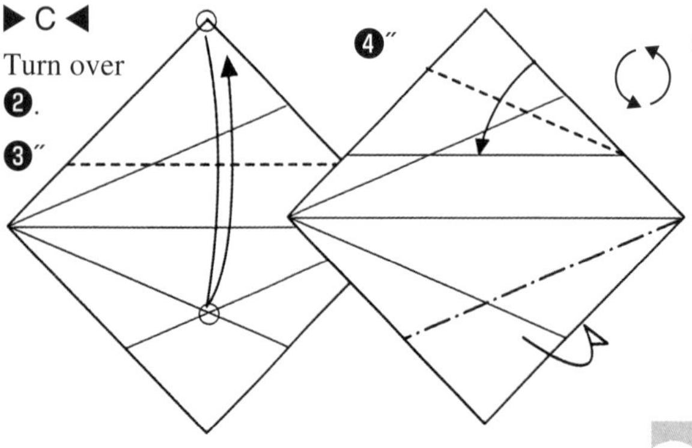

❺″

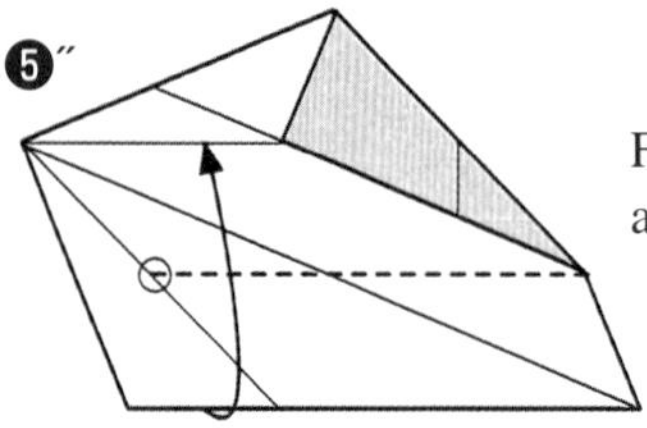

Fold in the same way as B.

❻″ (×16)

See page 94 for the joining method of C.

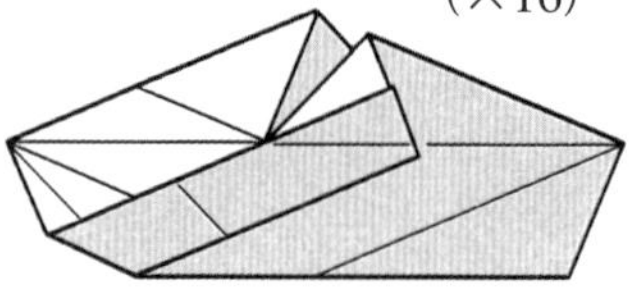

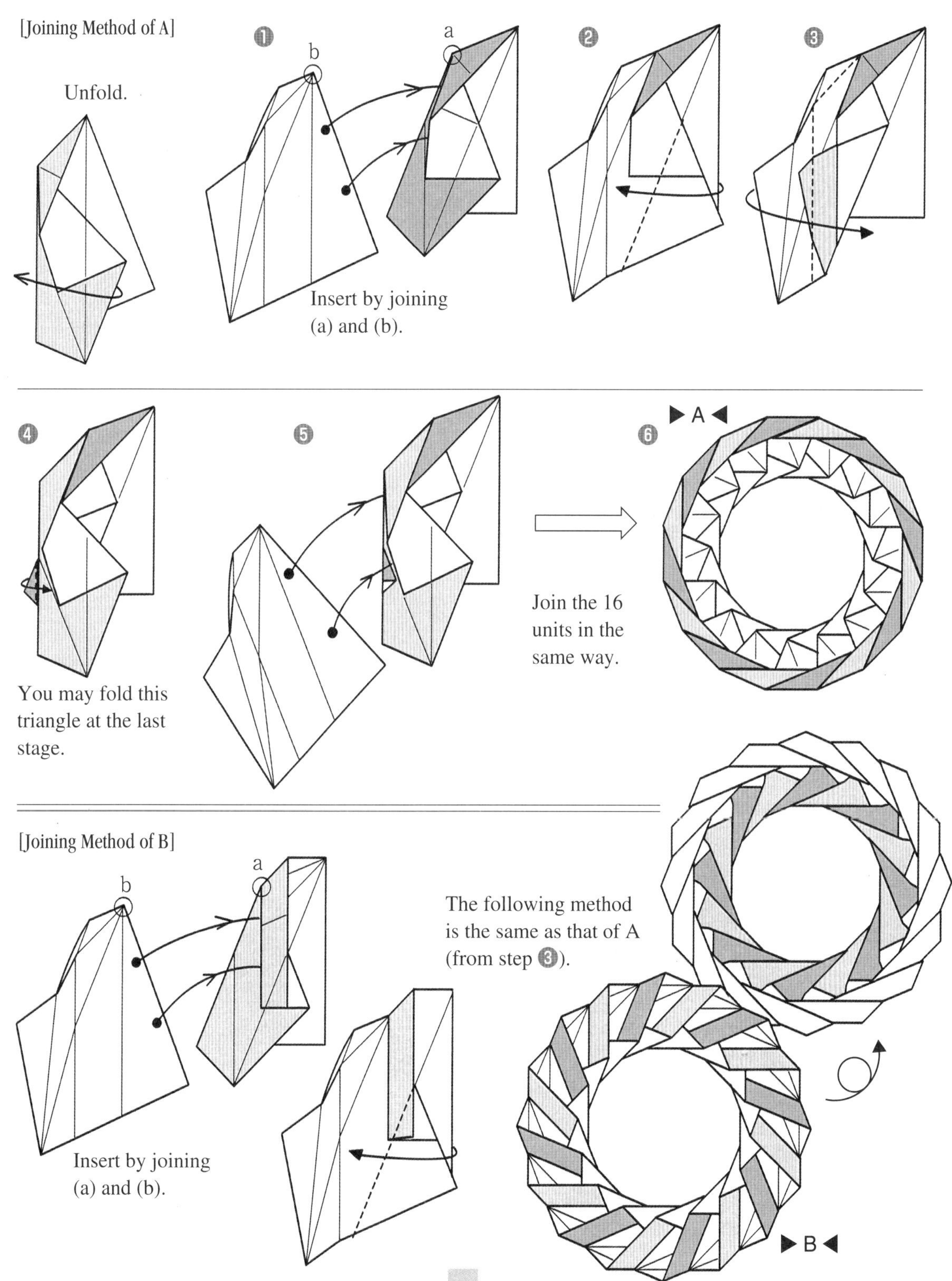
[Joining Method of A]
Unfold.
1
b
a
Insert by joining
(a) and (b).
2
3
4
You may fold this
triangle at the last
stage.
5
6
▶ A ◀
Join the 16
units in the
same way.
[Joining Method of B]
b
a
Insert by joining
(a) and (b).
The following method
is the same as that of A
(from step 3).
▶ B ◀

[Joining Method of C]

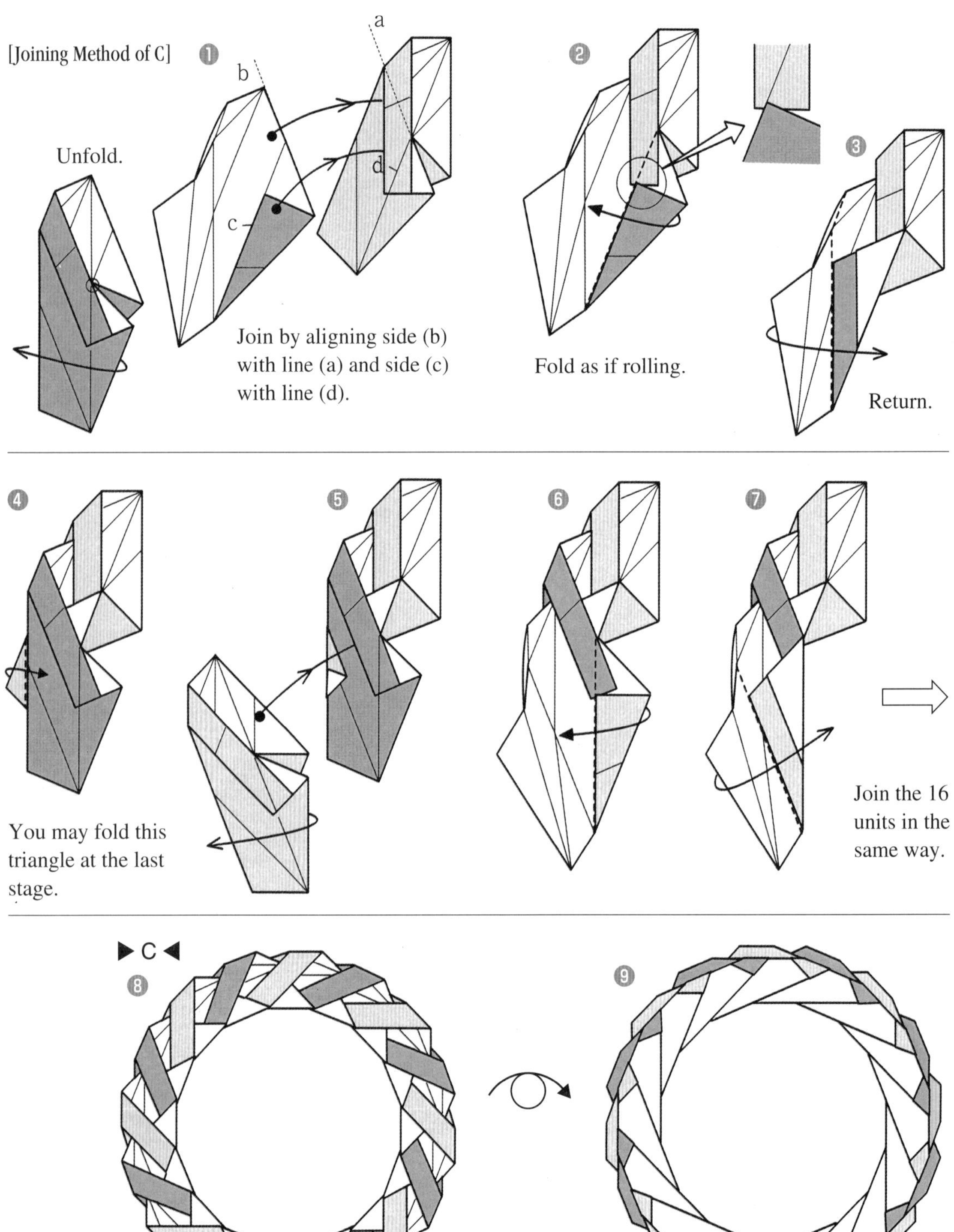

# ORIGAMI RINGS

This collection of fascinating rings has a variety of uses for Christmas decorations, brooches, earrings and other ornaments.
But these are not the goals of this unit origami. The very essence is the pleasure of folding, joining and completing the rings.
It is also interesting to enjoy the dramatic changes of impressions which brought about by different color arrangements.
Introduced in this book are 28 kinds of rings.
The simple and clear instructions are so easy to follow that even absolute beginners can make units in a few steps without confusion.
There are not many units to make, so you can readily get to work. They will reveal a kaleidoscopic world of rings.